MONTESSORI CLASS MANAGEMENT

by
Franco Albanesi, A.M.I.

ADAMS PRESS
CHICAGO, ILLINOIS

Library of Congress
Catalog Card Number 90-83194

ISBN 0-9628008-0-5

The Albanesi Educational Center
Publisher

Contents

About the Author

Franco Albanesi is a self-made individual currently working with his wife as Montessori Curriculum Consultant to school administrators, teachers and parents.

After receiving his Montessori training in Europe during the mid '60s (first in London, England and later in Bergamo, Italy), he and his wife gained much of their teaching experience and excellent reputation by team-teaching.

In 1974 the Albanesi Educational Center was established as a Montessori school for children 2½ to 13 years of age. Soon, two separate schools spawned from the Center and grew to independent status. The Contemporary Montessori Education (CME) Training Program, another offspring of the Center, is today a fully independent institute and operates on-going training programs in Montessori education on a year-round basis.

In recent years, the creation of Montessori curriculum programs and didactic printed materials offered through lectures and workshops to Montessori schools everywhere has claimed national and international recognition for Mr. and Mrs. Albanesi. Both are often invited to speak at Montessori schools and at national Montessori conferences around the country.

Mr. Albanesi is an active contributor of articles to Montessori publications around the world.

Foreword

This manual is dedicated to parents and teachers seeking to discover how intelligence can be positively influenced and increased through pedagogical efforts. By defining intelligence as *the ability of making rational abstractions* we can understand why our goal in education is to supplement genetic conditions with a rationally prepared educational environment. The preparation of the educational environment is perhaps the most important factor that adults have at their disposal today to ensure the development of critical thinking in children.

Teaching children to distinguish truth from falsehood, facts from opinions, the possible from the impossible is tantamount of developing individuals who are mentally healthy, psychologically secure and emotionally fulfilled. To achieve this goal we must be committted to value rationality as the highest motivating factor of our life. It is in this way that we come to understand that integrity does not imply sacrifice, that virtue is not painful and that non-contradictory pleasure is the only true form of reward.

The welcome consequence of such an awareness is manifested in the world through the spreading of more rational forms of education, more cooperative relationships among people, more productive, creative and rewarding exchanges and ultimately a widespread revolution in human consciousness.

Montessori training programs everywhere should find this *class management manual* essential in the preparation of their teachers. While the teaching of the use of the Montessori didactic materials constitutes the major portion of a Montessori training program, a systematic study of the pedagogy of rational relationship for class management is commonly entirely neglected. My experience of over 20 years in Montessori education consistently indicates that the shortcomings of education are fundamentally the shortcomings of the spiritual preparation of the teachers and of the adults who do the educating. The world does not suffer so much from the lack of teachers, as it does from the lack of good ones. Better teachers are those who have traded prejudice for objectivity, whim for reason, despotism for affection, permissiveness for guidance, power for respect and dullness for alert observation.

Better teachers can only be found amongst those who have committed themselves to learning how to be more and more rational in their relationship with children.

This manual represents an effort directed at galvanizing people in education to consider the study of the pedagogy of rational relationship as indispensable for the creation of *good* teachers. Without them, the future history of mankind will continue to be dominated by conflict and contradiction, because we are currently educating people to relate with one another and with nature at large, in a most destructive way. We are teaching people that short range advantages outweigh long range disadvantages; that individuals are unimportant in themselves and that they are important only if they serve the group, society or the state. The main message of traditional education has been that there is no reward in being an integrated individual, but there is great security and pleasure in belonging to a group, there is power in numerical majority and that right and wrong are mere by-products of force and conformism.

Introduction

New and experienced teachers alike can find anticipating the difficulties of the first days of school quite a challenge. A teacher is a master planner. The teacher must engineer the classroom environment to meet the needs of three distinct groups of people: the children, their parents and the rest of the school staff members (administrators, assistant teachers, other teachers). Each group has needs entirely different from the others.

By environment we should understand not only the physical surroundings, but also and especially our own psychological preparation, our own mental attitudes and philosophy of education. Thus, the preparation of the environment includes the order and cleanliness of the furnishings and equipment as well as the order and awareness of the teacher's mind. The teacher, with his or her mental attitudes, affects in great part the attitudes, motivation and values of the students. Disciplined children are the result of a conscious kind of guidance on the part of the teacher. Such a guidance is possible if the teacher understands that all motivation comes from a value system. When a child is disruptive or unmotivated in the work, the teacher should question himself as follows:

What are the values of this child?
Can I verbalize them explicitly to the child?
Can we both be aware of how different my values are
    from his?
Can his values be respected?
Can my values be understood by the child?
What do my values offer the child?
Can we exchange values, barter, negotiate in mutual agree-
    ment and satisfaction?

The human being cannot exist without the process of education. Such a process takes place whether we formalize it or not.

Formal education is designed to achieve specific results by using a well-planned *curriculum* and applying a *method*. Method and curriculum rely very much on the understanding of *principles* and *techniques* for their effectiveness. The Montessori method offers an alternative to the traditional system.

While the traditional system is based primarily on *regimenting* the students to meet the dictates of the curriculum, the Montessori method seeks to operate on the environment and the curriculum to make sure that it is *adapted* to the needs of the individual student. The former is based on force and authority; the latter recognizes the intrinsic biological interaction that must exist between the mind of the individual student and the preparation of the educational environment in order to achieve non-contradictory and integrated competence at living.

The study presented here is an attempt to urge others (particularly those conducting Montessori training courses) to ask what has been neglected for so long in educating young minds. It is my contention that integrity is not possible without rational thinking and that both are values that have to be taught and learned. Humanity cannot afford to let integrity or rational thinking flourish by chance (as it is currently happening). Educators have no choice but to take up this study with eagerness, build their own rational abstractions and learn to guide a whole new generation of teachers to incorporate the study of rational human relation in the everyday menu of their students' intellectual development. Defaulting on this basic responsibility will simply translate in failing as educators, no matter whether the traditional or the Montessori method is used.

By applying the pedagogy of rational human relationship we are forced to consider new alternatives, new creative ways that are non-contradictory in order to give children the opportunity of abstracting the truth about the importance of living with integrity.

The traditional approach has taught us two ways with which to deal with contradiction: through intimidation, power and force (the child must conform and do as he is told regardless of his understanding), or through permissiveness, where the child himself is despotic, spoiled, or plainly abandoned to his own resources. Both approaches are contradictory, because in both cases *force*, not *intelligence*, operates. In a thousand variations, often disguised as faith, love, trust, respect, we have taught children to fear, not to understand. Subtly and more insidiously, the message of force has remained at the center of all motivation. Is there a motive that is not the result of fear, force or intimidation? Can it be the sole motive acceptable in a rational form of education? If we answer yes to both of these questions, we are on the way to discovering a true alternative approach, not another variation of the old, not another contradictory system.

The important lesson to learn is: "It is rational to pursue non-contradictory pleasure." All children want to pursue pleasure, but theirs is often contradictory; in the long run, it produces pain. Can children learn this lesson through *intelligence*, without force? Can we teach the great lesson on the value of rationality without contradictions? Can we do it in a non-Machiavellian way, so as to make sure that the end does not justify the means? What words, what verbalizations would be appropriate for us to learn so as the children's deepest understanding would be awakened to absorb and embrace effortlessly this concept of self-discipline?

The educator is now delivered from all models, from all stereotyped methods and formulas. Now the educator performs his true function *only* if he/she is creative, using one's mind as an artist would use the paint brush and palette. The teacher must speak to the child's inner sense and find agreement between the inner and the outer, between desire and reality and both must come out with the same observation, the same understanding and the same abstraction. If this is done, both the adult and the child will have come to experience a new form of education in which intelligence is the natural outcome.

There is biological dependence and psychological dependence. Biological dependence is part of life. As we live, we depend on food, clothing and shelter. Psychological dependence is a neurosis. Can we live without having to be psychologically damaged, psychologically dependent? Can our children be raised psychologically secure? And what kind of educational approach would ensure that they learn to be independent and psychologically secure?

The mind demands security. We must have order and sanity to live happily. The baby must receive affection, protection and comfort in order to grow up without trauma, without damages. Why do we change our approach towards the children at one point or another? When do we say to the child: "That's enough affection; that's enough protection. Now you must be on your own. Now you must be prepared for the 'real' world. Now you must be independent?" How can we distinguish between affection and responsibility? Is affection unconditional? Do we say: "I love you so much, you can do anything you want?"

The small child wants candy. He has tasted how delicious it is and now he demands it. What do I do? How do I know what affection is? Can affection go hand in hand with intelligence? Intelligence says that despite the emotions, there is a necessity for mapping out the route of action by taking into consideration both the short range and the long range effects. Thus, intelligence must be based on rationality, on sanity. It must have its roots in what is non-contradictory.

Our study of the pedagogy of relationship shows that maintaining communication is the first and the last step in educating rationally. How do we do this? The child who demands to eat candy, for example, is posing a challenge of communication to us. How do we meet it?

The steps of rational communication might be summed as follows:

a) *verbalization of feelings* to establish the same emotional level (listen for a YES)

An adult could verbalize a child's feelings like this:

"You really love the taste of candy, don't you?"

"Candy is so delicious, isn't it? I love the taste, too."

b) *stating expectations that are reasonable* and consonant to the context (designed to give an appropriate *choice of behavior*)

An adult could give a child guidance and opportunity for making choices by saying:

"Children want candy whenever they wish, but adults must decide *if* and *when* children can have candy. I have decided to allow one piece of candy after dinner for a well-behaved child only."

"There are two behaviors you can choose from:
1) Throw a temper-tantrum and get no candy now or after dinner;
2) Compose yourself and get ready for dinner now, so that you may have a piece of candy after dinner;
Which of these two behaviors do you prefer?"

This approach to communication is taking into consideration all the possible issues and implications. It maps out the events and situations that one may encounter as though one was taking a journey. It is a way of considering the child's feelings without condemning them or accepting them. It is a way of considering the context of the kind of relationship we experience. It is a way of considering both the short range and the long range consequences.

Rational communication is the only way to educate children in the acquisition of psychological independence and psychological security. It is in this way that the child may arrive at an *objective evaluation of oneself: SELF-ESTEEM.*

Principles of Pedagogy

Some of the principles or laws that govern a rational form of education can be identified as follows:

1) HUMAN VALUES ARE BASED ON PLEASURE/PAIN JUDGMENTS.
It is an inescapable law that we all seek pleasure and avoid pain. The child is no exception. It is through the senses that abstract thinking and value judgments are formed. All abstractions that adhere to reality must be logically reducible to the sensorial level.

2) MOTIVATION IS DICTATED BY THE PROSPECT OF GAIN.
The adult's work is often motivated by concrete, outer results. The work of the small child differs. It is primarily dictated by inner needs for the construction of the physical and mental personality. The former is a conscious gain; the latter is a subconscious gain.

3) NATURAL HUMAN DEVELOPMENT OCCURS THROUGH MENTAL ORDER.
The human mind naturally seeks to organize, classify and integrate the sensorial experiences derived from the environment. Dr. Montessori suggested that adults be not too concerned with the inner, "secret" processes of integration within the child. The preparation of the educational environment on the other hand, ought to receive our utmost attention. If the environment is clean, attractive, orderly, warm and rationally prepared, it will provide the sustenance on which a healthy, natural development takes place.

4) RESPECT FOR INDIVIDUAL SELF-PACED LEARNING FOSTERS A COOPERATIVE ADULT/CHILD RELATIONSHIP.

The small child's own pace of learning, often unrelated to results, is recognized in the Montessori method as having developmental biological functions in its own right. A learning environment or a curriculum that does not violate the self-paced process of the individual produces a healthy attitude towards learning and a cooperative relationship between the adult and the child. The traditional system, on the other hand, so frequently and universally violates this principle that people have become accustomed to seeing children criticized impatiently, their independence and dignity taken away, often even punished for failing to conform or to keep up with the pace of learning.

This practice is so widespread that it can be viewed in its devastating effects at all levels: be it a mother interfering with her child's desire to practice a suitable activity by doing it instead for the child *faster*, or be it the school professor demanding that the "slow" student catch up with the rest of the class somehow, miraculously.

5) FREEDOM IMPLIES COMPETENT AND RESPONSIBLE LIVING.

The concept of freedom without responsibility simply translates into *license* and disorder. A method based on this concept of education will produce ill-developed individuals. By emphasizing responsibility at the expense of freedom, we produce *repressive authority*. Again, the results of such a method cannot be in harmony with mental health.

A great deal of conflict, hostility or rebelliousness has its roots in repression and loss of freedom. The Montessori method views freedom as order within the mind and reflected in personal comportment outwardly. Therefore, freedom is not just desire to do what one likes, but the rational response to each challenge of life. Such liberty is a necessary prerequisite for developing intelligence.

6) THE LEARNING PROCESS IS BIOLOGICALLY BUILT-IN AND REQUIRES NO REWARDS OR PUNISHMENTS FOR ITS OPTIMUM FUNCTIONING.

As the heart beats spontaneously, so the intellect naturally functions by sorting out, comparing and abstracting through the sensory experiences received. Lack of curiosity, boredom, misbehavior are biologically appropriate responses to an environment that does not meet the needs of the individual child. Rewards serve only to mask the real cause of the deviation, while punishment creates inner conflict and neurosis about the entire process of learning.

Identifying Terms

EDUCATION — is the active *process* of the human mind engaged at recognizing and abstracting the facts of reality to be used for one's competence at living. Education may be *formal* or *informal*, but it is an essential process to the functioning of the human mind, therefore education occurs both consciously and subconsciously. Humans do not have a choice to be or not to be educated, since choices are themselves secondary products of education.

CURRICULUM — is a logically organized path or course of study of one or more branches of education. A curriculum can only apply to *formal* education. A curriculum for informal education is a contradiction in terms, since informal education happens without previous considerations, experience or goals.

METHOD — is an approach, a manner in which a curriculum of a specific branch of education is presented in the art of learning and of teaching. A method is the product of discoveries and successful applications of educational principles and techniques.

PRINCIPLE — is a basic law or truth. A principle is universal and it does not admit exceptions. A principle is in adherence with nature, reality and must be non-contradictory. A principle operates regardless of human judgment.

TECHNIQUE — is a procedure to be applied with discretion. A technique, to be effective, must be applied by considering its relationship to principles and the variables of context.

Successful techniques adhere to the principles of reality; they are contextual, they are dictated by logic, and they admit exceptions.

MONTESSORI — is a method of formal education. It is based on scientific observation as a principle of discovery and on rationality as the standard for all its applications and techniques.

Classroom Management Techniques

Although the principles of rational education are essential and must be understood thoroughly, it is with class management techniques that one must begin when working in the classroom.

The management techniques developed in this program have been isolated from the personality of the teacher and presented at the beginning of this course, because student-teachers, though not requested to take initiative in class interaction, must nonetheless be ready to meet the children in the classroom at a minimum level of interaction. Their awareness of the class management techniques that are routinely used by the Montessori Guide prevents unnecessary errors in relating with the children and provides the essential background needed to profit in their educated observation of their role model.

The student-teacher should become a keen observer of the principles and techniques that govern the interactive relationship between students and Montessori Guide. From this observation, the student-teacher learns to apply the correct techniques of right relationship by considering *rationality* as the standard and by considering the actual context of each arising interactive situation.

1. Anticipation

The act of thinking ahead is the act of anticipating. This technique is so widely necessary in education that it often acts like a principle.

With a specific goal in his mind, the teacher must be prepared to paint a picture of exactly what the child will be able to do after the lesson. The picture should portray the difficulties the child will encounter and show him how to overcome such difficulties by filling him with triumphal anticipation.

By using consistently this technique, the teacher becomes extremely communicative, and the child learns the mental processes so necessary for independent thinking and decision making.

Anticipation can be defined as the process of thinking that focuses on possible obstacles in reaching a goal.

VERBALIZATION EXAMPLE

The teacher is planning to take out the class to the playground.

LESS RATIONAL
(without anticipation)

The teacher rings the bell and says: "It's time for us to put away the work we are doing and go outside. When everyone is ready, we can line up and go."

As soon as the teacher finishes her announcement, the children rush to put their work away. Materials are sloppily replaced on the shelves. Objects are forgotten and left behind in the haste. Children have accidents and bump into one another frequently causing easy altercations. Some rush to the door to be first in line to go out.

MORE RATIONAL
(with anticipation)

The teacher rings the bell and says: "I'll be coming around to whisper some words in your ears. I'll look for those children who are carrying on with their activities and are not disturbing anyone."

Whispering — "Kellie, you may put your work away. I'll be watching how carefully you replace everything, how you walk and if you can sit down at your table ready to be called to go outside. Do you think you can do all that?"

Child: "Yes."

2. Preparation of Environment

The concept of preparing the environment for a special event or for the next stage of development is not a new idea. In fact, it is an invention of nature. Dr. Montessori, as any scientifically trained researcher soon finds out, observed this biological phenomenon repeat itself in all the manifestations of life. By simply applying nature's precept to the education of children, Dr. Montessori merely demanded that humans continue the work that nature has begun and not contradict it.

If the school is the place of learning where the intellect of the child is to be exposed to the wonders of academic subjects and social development, how then should this environment be prepared in order to fulfill its promise?

Perhaps, owing to its roots in ancient civilizations (where the authority of the elders was not to be questioned), the message of the traditional system has been consistently the same: teachers give classes, and students vie with each other to be recognized and graded successfully. Group-oriented learning is the cornerstone of the traditional system. Holding the group — not the individual — in mind we can see that our school environments have indeed been prepared to process the masses, certainly not to educate individuals.

In the traditional system, all preparations are meant for the benefit of the school administration and the teachers. None are there for the individual students. A classroom may have few or no windows, since they would be usually considered a distraction to both students and teachers during a lesson. The typical seating arrangement in rows of desks is prepared to accommodate a large number of students that can all be easily faced and controlled by the teacher.

For the convenience of specialized teachers, the curriculum has been broken down into seemingly endless fragments of knowledge called courses. Each class hour is conducted by a different teacher, and each hour is regimented by ringing bells indicating when to begin and when to end the study of a subject. (I not only refer to schools of higher education, where a minimum amount of curriculum compartmentalization and specialization is in order, but also to grade schools and even preschool programs that often "boast" the use of separate classes with separate teachers for each subject!)

From compulsory attendance to test scores, from homework to term papers, the traditional system has convinced us all, over the centuries, that fulfilling requirements, adapting to the group and the schedules, making the effort of fitting in, conforming (almost blindly) and being regimented is the legitimate price of becoming educated!

Following the principle that *rationally prepared school environments foster a rational approach to life*, serious educators have no choice but recognize that the mass-oriented and pressure-to-conform infested traditional system has for centuries actively contributed to "educate" people in the achievement of irrational and neurotic life styles. Today, the value of a so-called education (training is a better word) lies entirely in the smattering of academic and technical information that students are capable of acquiring, a task that consistently is best accomplished by vocational and specialized technical schools.

Although training — not education — is the legitimate term that schools ought to use in preparing students to acquire a trade or profession, the traditional system has confused one term for the other for so long that people often speak about one concept when they had in mind the other, and vice versa. We must eliminate this confusion for ourselves in order to communicate clearly.

There is a rational hierarchy of values in perfect agreement with reality that must be respected. Education comes first because its goal is intelligence (defined as non-contradictory living); training comes next because its goal is the mastery of a specific skill or profession. Education implies *competence at living*, while training implies *competence at earning a livelihood*. From education we can select the most appropriate training in harmony with our individual preference, but from specialized training we are not instructed about the value of integrity. Learning a trade does not imply learning the art of living rationally.

An intelligent or educated electrician is both an honest man and a well-versed professional. On the other hand, an uneducated individual lacks the very foundations that permit integrity and competence at living. Such a person is more likely

9

to be influenced by irrational and corrupt methods, which in turn will affect adversely one's competence and creativity even in the profession chosen for earning a livelihood.

In an endless effort to stumble onto a perfect blend, the traditional system, from preschool to college, under the vigilant guidance of "expert" educators and politicians, relentlessly reshuffles a combination of some or all of the following ingredients: discipline, regimentation, relaxation, subservience, worship, hypocrisy, conformism, stimulus and apathy. In this general unprincipled ambiance, one thing that the system consistently does not seem to be able to provide is education.

Principles of non-contradictory living, of integrity, creativity and intelligence are simply omitted from the curriculum. Moreover, results as to the efficacy of the academic courses which provide professional training (an area where the traditional system is presumably the strongest) are far from being satisfactory.

It will be a consciously prepared environment that can ensure the implementation of *rationality as the highest moral value of man.* The Montessori method of education, with its biological and scientific legacy, lends itself as the most viable pedagogical tool available today.

At variance with the traditional system, the Montessori classroom is prepared to meet the needs of each individual student without asking that the student adapt to it. By fulfilling the needs of the individual, we educate children to pursue their vocations for their own sake, not to serve the needs of society at the expense of the needs of the individual. As the learning process is respected and encouraged, the student's acquisition of knowledge is not pitted against honesty, integrity and rationality. In this way, education and training may be acquired without conflict.

VERBALIZATION EXAMPLE

Learning to make appropriate choices within a certain context is undisputedly an important aspect of competence at living rationally (intelligence). A typical traditional classroom offers little opportunity for making choices. The need for power and authority is thus justified by traditional educators as a necessary evil in teaching discipline to young children.

In a Montessori classroom, where independence and inner discipline are recognized to be more appropriate qualities than conformism in developing mature and responsible adults, the environment is consciously prepared to offer a great many opportunities to encourage the small children to make choices on a daily basis.

LESS RATIONAL
(Fostering conformism)

Teacher
(Speaking to the class)
Today I forgot to bring back my story book for the reading time. We can fill our last ten minutes' time in a different way. Which would you like to choose among these?

a) reading another book;
b) drawing and coloring;
c) singing song;

Children
(All speaking at the same time)

— Yea! Let's read another book!
— I want to draw pictures.
— Let's not sing song!
— Teacher, may I color?
— I don't want to hear another story
— I want to listen to a new story.

MORE RATIONAL
(Fostering independence)

Teacher
(Speaking to the class)
Today I forgot to bring back my story book for the reading time. We can fill our last ten minutes' time in a different way.

I will look for those children who are sitting at their tables very nicely and respectfully and I will come around to ask them what activities they may want to choose from the classroom shelves.

Do you have something in mind?

Child
Yes, I would like to draw a picture.

Teacher
You may get up and get the materials you need.

11

Teacher
So many suggestions!
We are going to have to put this issue to a vote.

Raise your hand if you want to listen to another story.

Raise your hand if you prefer to draw and color.

Raise your hand if you want to sing songs.

Well, the majority wants to listen to a new story.

Children
—Oh! I don't want to.
—I hate to listen to another story!
—I wanted to color.

Do you have something that you prefer doing?

Child
Yes. I would like to use the templates and decorate my poster.

Teacher
OK, you may go ahead. And you?

Child
I would like to help clean the hamster cage with Stephen.

Teacher
Will you be able to work together respectfully?

Children
Yes.

3. Isolation of Difficulties

A challenge is big only because its steps are not isolated. Instead, they appear combined and present themselves all at one time. A child may be easily overwhelmed by large challenges and give up easily.

Learning to isolate difficulties is a valuable technique in teaching children. It provides plenty of encouragement and much needed stamina to perserve and continue the task to its full completion. The essential aspect to remember about this technique is that its application requires that we become skillful at breaking down a complex problem into its simpler components. Of all the single parts, the first is the most central and most important aspect of the problem so that all the other parts may naturally be resolved.

VERBALIZATION EXAMPLE

A student presents an extemporaneous composition filled with punctuation, capitalization and spelling errors.

LESS RATIONAL
(no isolation of difficulties)

Teacher
I marked all the places where you must make your corrections. The circles tell you that you did not use capitalization properly. The little circles show the wrong or missing punctuation, and the x's tell you that you must check the dictionary to spell the words correctly.

Child (age 7)
I don't feel like doing all this.

Teacher
How are you going to learn to write, young man?

MORE RATIONAL
(isolating difficulties)

Teacher
You wrote a long story and I am glad. Now we must make the corrections. There are corrections in punctuation, in capitalization and spelling.

Child (age 7)
I don't feel like doing all this.

Teacher
It is a lot of correcting, isn't it?

Child
Yes.

Teacher
Shall we do just a few today? Which would you prefer to do today?

Child
I'll do the punctuation.

Teacher
That's sounds like a good start.

4. Self-Correction

The authenticity of Montessori materials used in a classroom is measured by the degree in which they conform to certain requirements needed for the development of independence, inner discipline and abstraction. Above all, Montessori materials differ from toys and other educational tools because they incorporate consistently some essential characteristics. In general, Montessori materials are:

- concrete and manipulative
- attractive and stimulating
- graduated in difficulty
- re-usable and designed for repetition
- built to size for the child's age
- suitable for isolating difficulties
- self-correcting

The last of these characteristics is discussed here as an important pedagogical technique. We shall see that its application can prove to be very useful, especially when the teacher must ask children to make corrections on their work.

Correcting children in their behavior and their work is an inseparable aspect of any adult in general and of a teacher's job in particular. Since correction implies exposing inadequacies and errors, self-esteem is inevitably placed in jeopardy.

One of the ways in which we learn to form an opinion about ourselves, particularly in childhood, has a lot to do with the way other people, especially other meaningful adults, hold us in regard. If, for example, as a child, I feel that my parents are frequently dissatisfied with my performance, be it behavioral or academic, I identify myself as being inadequate, incompetent or in some way lacking in value. My self-image will reflect both the opinion that others have of me and the opinion I have of myself. It is in this way that correction and criticism may lead to severe self-esteem damage.

Although no responsible adult deliberately over-criticizes a child's performance at the expense of self-esteem, correcting mistakes remains a delicate task that must be carried out notwithstanding. Concluding that all correction is detrimental is as untrue as believing that any form of correction is necessary and justifiable. The solution of this controversy lies not in whether we ought to correct or not to correct, but simply in *how* adults decide to carry out such an unsavory task.

Adults, particularly teachers, often come across to children as overpowering zealots, eager to teach a lesson, to explain, to test their knowledge and, of course, to correct. It is no wonder that so many children grow up suspicious about the real purpose of learning, and uncomfortable with academic subjects.

The aspect of self-correction that many Montessori materials display so brilliantly (the knob cylinders, for example, can only fit in their corresponding sockets by length and diameter) provide the opportunity for the children to experience the learning process without the constant presence of a seemingly omniscient adult who is there to measure their performance. Instead, by working independently and at their own pace, the children in a Montessori classroom are permitted to satisfy their natural curiosity and commit as many errors as they need in order to arrive at the correct procedure and the correct results. In such instances, the learning process is as spontaneous and self-gratifying as it is drinking cool, fresh water from a mountain spring on a hot summer day.

Is it possible to give children this type of learning experience instead of making it a painful ordeal for them?

The role of the adult in guiding the child through curiosity and exploration is to prepare an environment conducive to achieving the correct results. Exploration does not imply endless, chaotic experimentation. When the child explores, the adult has to decide whether the child is using the prepared environment in a constructive or destructive manner. If the child, for example, decides to use the Montessori materials in idleness and entertainment, the teacher will recognize that form of exploration as destructive. If the child uses the materials in a prescribed manner, the teacher will know that such an approach will lead the child to discovery and constructive results.

Toys, on the other, fulfill an entirely different purpose in the development of a child. Unlike the Montessori materials, they are designed for the so called "free play," precisely because they respond to random, imaginative play-acting. What the

16

child "discovers" from these activities are various forms of associations and fantasies.

Perhaps a child can play with toy cars for as long as 20 years, but he will definitely stop when he is able to substitute the imaginary toy car with a real car that he can finally drive himself down the street. This is how one uses imagination as a surrogate for reality.

The purpose of play is to give the child a mental experience, through imagination, of what he cannot have in reality. As soon as the child can have the experience in reality, and not just in his mind, he loses interest in play-acting and ultimately abandons it altogether.

Correction has no part in play-acting, because the child's fantasy is free to adhere completely to the images and results created by his imagination. The discovery and learning process, on the other hand, is quite different; its validity is not dictated by the child's imagination, but by objective results in reality.

The concept of self-correction in the Montessori environment is applied consistently through the use of the materials and the pedagogical preparation of the teacher in relating to children.

VERBALIZATION EXAMPLE #1

LESS RATIONAL
(damaging self-esteem)

Teacher
I have checked your composition and found many spelling mistakes. You need to check the dictionary and correct all the words I marked in red. Then, I want you to write this composition over without any spelling errors.

Child (age 8)
I hate compositions.

MORE RATIONAL
(enhancing self-esteem)

Teacher
In this first sentence I found a word that needs to be corrected. Can you bring me the dictionary and be a detective with me?

Child (age 8)
Yes.

Teacher
Let's see . . . What are the first three letters of this word, can you guess? Let's see if we can find this word in the dictionary. Oh, you found the right page. Let's see who is the first one of us to spot the word. It should be in this row.

Great! You saw it first! You can write it right above the misspelled one on your paper.

Shall we play this detective game with another word?

Child
Yes.

Teacher
Here is another misspelled word in your composition.

This time I think I'll beat you in finding it in the dictionary!

Let's see . . . what are its first three letters? Can you find the right page?

Oh! You found the page already. Now, let's see if I can see it before you . . . Oh my! Again, you beat me!

I have to say, you are a very good detective with words.

Shall we do more?

Child
Yes, yes!

VERBALIZATION EXAMPLE #2

LESS RATIONAL

Teacher
Out of six addition problems you only got one right. Let me show you what you did wrong.

It looks like you don't quite understand how to carry numbers over to the next column. I hope you'll remember.

Tomorrow you must do this assignment over.

Child (age 7)
I don't like addition.

MORE RATIONAL

Teacher
There is a control chart on the shelf for these addition problems. You can bring the chart here and check your work yourself.

Child (age 7)
I didn't do too well. I only got one problem right!

Teacher
That tells us that we need to work on additions with carrying some more, doesn't it?

Child
Yes.

Teacher
Shall we do one problem together and see if we can get it right this time?

Child
OK.

19

5. Verbalization of Feelings

The teacher must become skillful with this technique because it is of the highest importance. Rational relationship is possible only through interpersonal visibility. When our feelings are unidentified by others, we experience a great sense of alienation or separateness. The child's need for visibility is a natural requirement for emotional development. Without satisfying this need, the individual may grow up with severe emotional inadequacies. The ability to identify and name one's own feelings is directly related to the way meaningful adults taught us as children how to express our emotions and how to care for our emotional needs.

One of the tragedies ensuing from the way people learned to identify their feelings incorrectly is reflected in their inability to communicate. It is through verbalizing people's feelings correctly that we as humans can be certain of mutual understanding. I know that I am understood by someone only when my feelings are accurately described.

The technique of verbalizing feelings begins with perceiving and identifying emotions correctly. Next, comes the ability of expressing and verbalizing that which is perceived, to see if the other person is responding affirmatively. One knows that someone's feelings are correctly verbalized, because the other person indicates through nodding or, more frequently, with a series of resounding "Yes!"

Perhaps the most difficult part of this technique, however, comes *after* we learn to verbalize someone's feelings. At this point we have to know what to do, or not do, with the feelings that we have brought to full awareness. I suspect this, at least in part, is the reason why most of us were not taught to verbalize and name feelings. Our parents and teachers quickly realized that it was not enough to know the names of their own feelings or those of others, but that the most arduous part was still to come, that there is a great skill to be learned in dealing with the feelings after they are exposed. In general, most of us were taught to express feelings indiscriminately, and even act on them, or simply repress them.

The technique of verbalizing feelings is valid only if we map out clearly for ourselves the ultimate purpose of such a communication. Unless we keep in mind that rationality is the standard for establishing a deeper, meaningful relationship, a sense of estrangement is inevitable.

Verbalizing a child's feelings must always produce a *YES*. If the child is not intimidated or condemned for what he feels, he will be happy to agree and confirm the feelings that have been verbalized. His feelings are now visible and that visibility prevents hypocrisy.

Hypocrisy is a psychological deviation which in Dr. Montessori's terms ought to be treated like an illness. It is by arriving at a YES (a code-word that stands for psychological visibility) that a rational, honest, not hypocritical relationship can take place.

VERBALIZATION EXAMPLE

LESS RATIONAL	MORE RATIONAL
(wrong identification)	(correct identification)

Mark (age 6)
This work is too hard for me.

Teacher
No it isn't. This is baby stuff. Let me show you how easy it is.

Mark
I don't like this work. I can't do it well. I keep tearing the paper.

Teacher
That's alright. We are all here to learn. Show me that you are a good sport. Try once more.

Mark (age 6)
This work is too hard for me.

Teacher
Yes, this is very hard work. Not everyone can do this. I bet you could not even make one more word, not even just one more like this.

Mark
This one is easy. This one I can.

Teacher
Show me the one you are having the most trouble with. Can you try?

Mark
Yes.

21

6. Describing Events

At times a child has learned to be invisible to the adult, as far as feelings, thoughts or actions are concerned. Between the various complexities of life, the personal responsibilities and demands of other relationships, some children, both in the school classroom and at home, can slip through unseen and unheard, to some extent. This situation provides the background for very poor communication.

The technique of probing for details rather than accepting general and vague explanations for a certain kind of behavior helps the adult obtain a clearer, more precise and realistic picture of a child's emotions, intentions and thoughts. The child who is becoming more visible to the adult has less anxiety, guilt or need to hide behind vagueness. Conversely, an adult who remains consistently unaware of underlying motives, emotions or intentions of children can not possibly help those children become competent and aware of themselves.

VERBALIZATION EXAMPLE

The teacher asked Greg if he could help Paul set up a floor rug and lay out the number cards for the bank game. Fifteen minutes later the children seemed to have a dispute. When the teacher arrived on the scene, the boys had placed a rug too small for all the cards they had; they had placed the cards in reverse order, and were fighting over who should be taking charge of the setting up.

LESS RATIONAL (accepting literally)	MORE RATIONAL (detailed descriptions)
Paul (age 7) He won't let me do anything.	*Paul* (age 7) He won't let me do anything.
Greg (age 7) I was going to give him this packet of cards to lay out.	*Greg* (age 7) I was going to give him this packet of cards to lay out.
Paul He did most of the cards and wouldn't give me a turn.	*Teacher* Let's see if we can work together in a cooperative manner. Let's start from the beginning. Greg, which rug do we need for the bank game?
Teacher I thought I asked that you help each other. I didn't ask that you boss each other. That rug is too small anyway. And that is not a good place to put it down. It's too close to the door. I guess I need to come and fix everything myself now!	*Greg* A big one.
	Teacher Yes. Where is a good place for it?
	Greg Right in that corner, away from everyone.
	Teacher Excellent! Paul, can you put the smaller rug away while Greg lays out the big one?

Paul
Yes.

Teacher
Can you put down the first packet
of number cards?

Paul
Yes.

Teacher
Greg, describe to me what you
will be doing while Paul is busy
laying out the first batch of cards.

Greg
I'll be waiting for him to finish.
Then can I do the next packet?

Teacher
Yes. But will you be able to wait
without interfering? Can each one
of you wait for the other to finish
his part before starting?

Boys
Yes.

7. Providing Choices of Behavior

Most of us were taught that we cannot really control our behavior. We may have been brought up with some specific patterns of behavior applicable to certain occasions and have accepted such patterns as part of our personality. If you are insulted, for instance, it is acceptable, natural and expected to retort with an insult. We do not think that we can actually have a choice of behavior depending on the abstractions we have previously made.

By teaching children that people have many options in selecting their behavior, we can study and observe what we mean when we use the word "misbehavior."

Behavior is learned formally or informally. Most of us use an informal (subconscious) approach in teaching children how to behave. When we were children we learned our behavioral patterns mostly informally ourselves, from the adults who surrounded us. With this technique we strive to teach behavior formally, with accurate procedures and presentations as though we were teaching a math lesson. To do this effectively, of course, it requires observation, study and thinking things through.

But behavior can and should be taught formally by parents and teachers. The problem is, what is the correct behavior that we want to teach? How do we know that one form of behavior is worth passing on to the children, while another should not be shown? In a rational form of education, which is the only valid form of education for the human being, the standard for the correct selection of behavior must be rationality and no other.

Patterns of behavior are learned by children for the same reason: psychological security. Each pattern is a defense mechanism. Children may develop patterns of aggressiveness, passivity, intimidation or whining, but in principle, all patterns are developed to achieve pleasure and to preserve one's satisfaction.

The difficulty for the educator is to teach children to respond to the challenges of life, not with a behavioral pattern, but with intelligence. A pattern can never be adequate for the ever changing contexts of life, but intelligence can tackle the principles, the laws of human relationship and respond correctly to each particular situation rationally.

To discover the most rational approach, we must be able to consider the fact that behavior can be selected among a variety of possibilities.

VERBALIZATION EXAMPLE #1

Tom (age 4) was taught to serve juice by placing the cup next to the napkin. Aaron (age 3) was taught that the cup should be placed on the napkin. When Tom serves, Aaron corrects him and tells him to put the cup of juice on the napkin. Tom becomes upset and disciplines Aaron by telling him that the juice should be put next to the napkin.

The rational goal that we as adults must teach children is flexibility, since it is just as rational to have juice on or off the napkin, the conflict is brought about by learned behavioral patterns that conflict with each other.

A choice of behavior can only be given when the child is receptive to understanding the value of making a choice. At the moment in which we observe the event, we probably have very little opportunity of changing the patterns. The teacher will learn that the pattern can be exposed and the conflict can be prevented. The children cling to their patterns because they are using them to preserve their value, their assertiveness and their competence. They have identified their self-esteem with the patterns they have learned.

Why would a child want to change a pattern of behavior with which he has identified his psychological security? The child uses the behavior pattern to boss, or control others, even if it means having conflict with others. But we must show him that his psychological security and integrity can be preserved *without* conflict, without having to boss or intimidate another. Therefore, the teacher must prepare the psychological conditions ahead of time (anticipation) in order to stop an irrational behavioral pattern and to allow intelligence to operate.

LESS RATIONAL

Teacher

Tom, yesterday you kept asking Aaron to keep his juice cup on the side of the napkin. Aaron wanted his cup on the napkin and you were very rude to him. Why do you cause such problems?

Tom

The juice cup should be on the table, not on the napkin. That's the right way to serve juice and Aaron wouldn't listen to me. He kept moving the cup on the napkin.

Teacher

Aaron doesn't like his cup on the table next to the napkin. He likes it on his napkin. Why can't you understand that? You need to learn to be flexible. Do you know what "flexible" means?

Tom

No.

Teacher

It means that some things that are not so important can be done in different ways. You can serve juice with the cup on the napkin or by the napkin and it doesn't make any difference one way or the other.

Tom

The right way to serve juice is to put the cup next to the napkin. Miss Franklin told me.

MORE RATIONAL

Teacher

Yesterday I noticed that you had problems with Aaron when you served juice. Can we talk about it?

Tom

Aaron won't listen to me. I tell him that the cup should be kept near the napkin, but he keeps moving it on the napkin. He makes me mad.

Teacher

Do you think it's not right to put the cup on the napkin?

Tom

Miss Franklin showed me how to serve juice. The cup must always go next to the napkin, not on the napkin. I told Aaron, but he won't listen.

Teacher

I see. You know, in my class it is not important if the cup goes next to the napkin or on the napkin. Aaron can choose if he prefers his cup to be placed on or off the napkin and I will be choosing children who can serve juice by giving this choice to the children. Do you like to be picked to serve juice?

Tom

Yes.

Teacher

Will you be able to give Aaron a choice as to where he wants his juice cup on the table without bossing him?

Tom
Yes.

Teacher
I am so glad. I hope next time I pick you there won't be an argument between you and Aaron about this. I can not choose children who cause arguments when they serve juice and crackers.

VERBALIZATION EXAMPLE #2

LESS RATIONAL (repeating informally learned behavioral patterns)	MORE RATIONAL (seeking to teach formal rational behavior)
Angela (age 6) Jay scribbled on my paper.	Angela and Jay complain about each other.
Jay (age 7) She made me ruin my work. She shakes the table so much.	*Teacher* What can you do, Jay, when Angela shakes the table?
Teacher You had better stop this complaining and learn to get along better. Go back to your seats and show me that you can be respectful with each other.	*Jay* I can ask her to stop.
	Teacher Will you stop shaking the table if Jay asks?
	Angela Yes. But he didn't ask.

Teacher

Jay, you have two ways you can choose from, when Angela shakes the table:

a) you can get mad and scribble her paper;

b) you can politely ask her to stop shaking the table.

Which do you prefer?

Jay

I prefer to ask her to stop politely.

Teacher

Do you know why you prefer that over the other?

Jay

Because if I get mad at her and scribble her paper she gets mad at me and it never ends.

Teacher

I hope Angela is going to be more careful with her table and apologize to Jay if she accidentally bumps the table. Can you do that, Angela, if it happens again?

Angela

Yes.

8. Dramatization

Sometimes it is valuable to know how to stimulate a child to initiate his or her interest in something. A lesson given without stimulus is like a boring story. Small children in particular respond so positively to lively dramatizations. They love relating drama to reality and they have great attraction for those teachers who are capable of using their imagination to enhance otherwise sterile tasks. This technique is widely incorporated throughout the Montessori materials which, though designed to educate, provide opportunities for ritualistic and slightly theatrical presentations.

VERBALIZATION EXAMPLE

LESS RATIONAL	MORE RATIONAL
(a dry, arid presentation)	(a lively, interesting lesson)

Teacher

This is the root of the plant, this is the trunk and this is the branch.

Show me the trunk.
Show me the branch.
Show me the root.

What is this?

Teacher

All plants have roots, a trunk and branches. Show me the trunk. Show me the root. Show me the branch.

I am going to turn the pictures over so you can't see them. I wonder if you can guess them.

Where is the picture of the . . . root?
Good!
See if you can find the branch.

Dramatization does not have to occur by supplying the child with an overwhelming amount of spoken detailed information. Small children can be easily distracted by too many words which, instead of helping, can be confusing. Dr. Montessori insisted that the teacher introduce new lessons to young children with a minimum of words. By pointing out the objects on the table, only the essential words — those designed to carry the concepts the young child would need to acquire — should be uttered: "This is *large*, large, large. This is *small*, small, small." This isolation of difficulty, if carried out with ritualistic perfection, elicits far more interest and concentration in the small child than wordy definitions and explanations on what is large and what is small.

9. Mirror Verbalization

This particular technique is derived from Haim Ginott,* author of some excellent books on child/adult relating. It is an approach of invaluable proportion both in the classroom and in the home. The adult must clearly establish the home or class community rule that children are protected from physical and emotional abuse. Interpersonal problems, therefore, may be brought to the attention of the adult who will not act as a judge, but specifically as a moderator whose *main goal is to reflect or mirror words and behavior from one party to the other.* By exposing each offender to the other, without taking sides, without condemnation or sympathy for either one, inevitably the two parties learn to look at each other through a wider picture, a wider context and therefore objectively. Only when the root of their conflict has clearly become exposed to each other, is a true resolution possible.

The self-evident, factual knowledge of events permits an objective, mutually agreeable solution to the problem. The value of this technique is so far reaching, it is not an exaggeration to claim that where its application has occurred consistently, we witness a deep transformation in the ability to relate rationally and objectively among children and adults alike.

In a case of complaint where one child accuses another for some offense, it seems so easy to respond automatically in favor of the alleged offended person and to jump to some hasty conclusion that the offender ought to be punished or taught a lesson.

"Coming for mirroring" does not have this specific goal. Its goals are objectivity and fairness, as well as the foundation for establishing ways to ensure good communication among people.

For this technique to be effective, both parties must be present when complaining about each other. The adult's role is not that of a judge but that of a mirror reflecting *verbatim*,

---

*Dr. Haim Ginott, *Between Parent and Child*, New York, N.Y., The Macmillan Company, 1956.

factually and unaltered the exact words of the children. Montessori teachers often call this the "bringing technique" and consistently observe how it dramatically diminishes the possibility for violence and antagonism in the classroom. Children learn, through this approach, that they are objectively protected. They learn this new way of solving their problems through correct verbalizations. They become more sensitive to one another and have little need to escalate a dispute into strong emotional rivalry or seek vengeance.

VERBALIZATION EXAMPLE

LESS RATIONAL (judgmental, partial, unfair)	MORE RATIONAL (factual, objective, fair)

Paul (age 11)
She hit me.

Teacher
Why did you do that?

Amy (age 12)
I didn't hit him.

Paul
Yes you did, and you know it!

Amy
Liar! He lies

Teacher
I think you should stop this nonsense and go back to your work. Just stay far from each other.

(The children leave as hostile to each other as they were. Neither one feels justice was done.)

Paul (age 11)
She hit me.

Teacher
Paul says you hit him.

Amy (age 12)
No, I didn't!

Teacher
Amy says she didn't hit you.

Paul
But she did. She poked her pencil at my neck while I was working.

Teacher
Paul says you poked your pencil at his neck while he was working.

Amy
I didn't know I did that. I just passed by his seat, and he became all upset with me.

Teacher
Amy says she just passed by your seat and you became all upset with her.

Paul
That's because she poked her pencil at me.

Teacher
Paul says he became upset because you poked your pencil at his neck.

Amy

I must have done that accidentally. I don't remember doing anything to him.

Teacher

Amy says she must have done it accidentally. Do you think that is possible?

Paul

I don't know. Maybe she did it accidentally, maybe she did it on purpose.

Amy

I don't even know that I have done anything.

Teacher

Paul, has that happened some other time that Amy comes to poke her pencil at you, or disturb you in any way?

Paul

No.

Teacher

Then, may we conclude that being the first time that this happens she may have done the poking inadvertently?

Paul

It's possible.

Teacher

Would you be satisfied if she appologized to you and promised to watch herself better in the future?

Paul

Yes.

Amy

I'm sorry.

10. Sitting Aside

Before one can apply the technique of "sitting aside" it is necessary to have a good knowledge of the principles of rational education.

The principle of cooperative relationship is based on mutual respect. Both the child and the adult must value objectivity and rationality as the standard of their relationship. Dealing fairly with the child and always providing the opportunity to express one's feelings non-destructively is very important for the establishment of a calm, peaceful atmosphere.

The technique of "sitting aside" should have nothing to do with a form of punishment, nor should it be associated with a "thinking chair" where the child broods over some wrong doing in repentance.

The request to sit aside should not come from the adult as an order or a demand, but as *an invitation to composure.* This technique is best applied in those cases when strong emotional reactions or outbursts may ensue. At the time of outburst we could say that the child is not in full possession of one's rational faculties. Time is needed for the child to "rest" and compose oneself before a verbal exchange is possible. Dr. Montessori speaks in her books of treating common emotional deviations such as anger, jealousy, envy, malice, antagonism as temporary illnesses to be "cured" with tenderness and care, certainly not by the use of punishment.

It is in this light that the technique of "sitting aside" should be viewed. By sitting aside the child has a chance to put distance between one's emotional turmoil and the event that triggered it. Through composure, encouraged by a non-intimidating teacher, the child's emotions can settle and the child becomes ready to re-assess disturbing actions and events more objectively and dispassionately.

Although the teacher asks the child to sit aside most politely, we must clearly understand that the teacher is by no means requesting the child's permission. Ideally, the teacher has the opportunity of presenting the request in the form of a choice of behavior that promptly gives the child an out from having to further escalate an emotional outburst.

For example, the teacher could say: "I see that you are very upset. Can you calm down and talk nicely or would you prefer to have a few minutes to sit aside and compose yourself?"

In this manner of talking, "sitting aside" becomes a form of communication — a way for the child to express one's intentions non-verbally.

The way a child responds to the teacher's invitation reveals a great deal about attitudes and intentions. The body language and non-verbal behavior have to be given great consideration in order to establish a mutually cooperative form of relationship. The child self-respect must always be preserved in order to ensure the basis for respect between child and adult.

If the child's hostility is specifically directed towards the adult, it is important that the adult have a clear plan in the effort of bringing the child out of his emotional outburst and into dispassionate objectivity. The child may not have the choice between throwing a bigger temper-tantrum and sitting aside. The choice is always between getting hold of his emotions on his own or receiving affectionate attention and guidance by sitting aside and resting in the presence of an adult in charge of looking after him.

As the child's behavior mellows by sitting aside, so does the body language of the child convey calmness and settlement. The child will have been instructed that when he is ready to return to normal, his manner of sitting will become composed naturally and consciously. His feet will be together, his hands will be kept properly folded in his lap, his body will rise straight and attentive, while his eyes will seek to meet the eyes of the teacher, communicating absolute readiness of the mind. Then the teacher will know that the time is right for conversing rationally about the events.

It is at this point that teacher and student will have the opportunity to talk calmly and agree together on better ways of dealing with similar situations in the future. Only then, the child, completely at rest and in control of his mental faculties, will receive permission to return to the normal activities that were interrupted by the outburst.

It is not necessary to have an emotional outburst of some kind in order to use this technique. Often, particularly in a well run Montessori class, children will ask to sit aside voluntarily, just to rest. In such a normalized classroom, the stigma of punishment will have completely vanished.

Some children, particularly small ones, may have difficulty, at first, understanding what sitting aside is all about. It is often the children themselves, even though the teacher may have taken great precautions in avoiding this, that associate sitting aside with a form of punishment. Whenever children are punished, inevitably, they retain hostility, and hostility is hardly a good companion of respect. Respectful relationships can never be built through hostility. It is absolutely necessary to remove all sense of hostility in the child while he/she is sitting aside, before any form of rational dialogue may take place between student and teacher.

How can this be achieved if the very act of sitting side is confused with punishment and becomes the very source of new hostility in the child? For sitting aside to be really effective and a successful form of communication, we must clearly understand that the role of the teacher in this technique is a matter of great subtlety, a real art. It is not merely the child that by sitting quietly must try to communicate respect, but it is the constant presence of the teacher, who is actively interacting with the child, that plays a great part in the final successful outcome. The teacher must encourage the child to show a respectful attitude by sitting quietly, with an erect posture and composed, ready to be invited for a brief conversation and agreement and then to join the rest of the class in normal activities.

The length of sitting aside is undetermined. It will be the child's attitude and the teacher's own judgment that will be the determining factors of its appropriate length.

VERBALIZATION EXAMPLE

Darren (age 5) knows that it is not acceptable to act silly and show off to attract attention in the class. The teacher has repeatedly warned Darren to stop that behavior. Darren stops temporarily only to begin again as soon as the teacher becomes involved with some other student. Eventually the teacher has no alternative and must ask him to sit aside.

LESS RATIONAL
(to punish)

Teacher
I have repeatedly asked you to stop this behavior, but you have ignored my warnings and you must sit aside.

Darren
Oh shocks! I hate sitting aside! Do I have to?

Teacher
Yes, and you will have to sit aside for a long time.

(The child sits aside, but with hostility.)

MORE RATIONAL
(to communicate)

Teacher
I can see that you are very excited and want to play a lot. I can no longer give you warnings. Perhaps by sitting aside next to me you can calm down.

Darren
Do I have to sit aside?

Teacher
Absolutely! And I want to see if you remember to sit properly, with your hands in your lap and your feet together. Tell me, do you wish to sit aside for a very long time or do you prefer to sit for just a short while?

Darren
I prefer to sit aside for just a short while.

Teacher
Well then, let me see how nicely you can sit right here. I'll watch you and call you back when I think you are ready.

(About five minutes later)

Teacher
I see that Darren has been sitting down very quietly and properly. Are you ready to go back to your seat?

Darren
Yes.

Teacher
But I wonder if you are going to act silly again and make everyone laugh. What do you think?

Darren
No, I have my work to do.

Teacher
What will happen if you start acting up again? What do you think we should do then?

Darren
I won't.

Teacher
But what are we going to do if you start again?

Darren
I'll have to sit aside for the rest of the day!

Teacher
I surely hope *that* won't have to happen.

11. Naming Issues

This technique is necessary when children have the tendency to argue. When you find yourself locked into a conversation with a child that does not go anywhere, it is important to name issues that clarify and focus people's attention.

Naming issues is also an important technique to enhance the visibility of both the child and the adult to each other. Without naming issues, we get into circular reasoning and have little hope for clarity. The basic gain of the child in establishing a multiplicity of issues is to try to pursue one's interests without having to pay the price or at the expense of the adult.

VERBALIZATION EXAMPLE

LESS RATIONAL	MORE RATIONAL
(circular reasoning, side-tracking)	**(naming issues)**

Teacher What are you doing, James?	*Teacher* What are you doing, James?
James (age 7) I was just putting my work away.	*James* (age 7) I was just putting my work away.
Teacher But why are you next to the teacher's cabinet?	*Teacher* It seems to me that you really wanted to do some art work with yarn and glue, don't you?
James I don't know.	*James* Yes.
Teacher What are all those pieces of yarn on your tray?	*Teacher* It is important that you ask me when you want something from the art cabinet. Perhaps you can do a project if you learn to ask me, instead of helping yourself without permission. Is that agreed?
James Someone put them there. I was just putting my work away.	
Teacher And why do you have a bottle of glue in your hand?	*James* Yes.
James Oh, that is from before. I was trying to put it back in your cabinet.	*Teacher* Good. Go ahead and put your work away. I'll put away the art stuff. Thank you.
Teacher But who takes these things out of my cabinet? I did not give anyone permission to get into my cabinet.	
James I don't know.	
Teacher Well, give me the yarn and glue. I'll put these things away. Please go back to your seat.	

12. Public Praising

This is an easy technique of minor importance. However, at times, it may prove to be quite useful.

Like all techniques, it should never be overused or abused. A child with low self-esteem or unmotivated often benefits from personal recognition. The delicate part about this technique lies in understanding that praises can cause damage, rather than benefit, when they do not adhere to the true feelings of the child.

To praise a child for something the child himself does not value *reduces visibility* instead of increasing it, thus producing guilt, hypocrisy or manipulation—the exact opposites of self-esteem. Public praising, therefore, must always reflect objectivity.

In this technique we must always keep in mind the difference between *subjective praises* such as "I like your work" and *objective praises* such as "You worked very hard on this, didn't you?" Subjective praises stress flattery and the desire to please; objective praises are factual, reality oriented, self-esteem oriented.

VERBALIZATION EXAMPLE

LESS RATIONAL
(subjective)

Teacher
My goodness, this is the best work I have ever seen! Your writing is so good. You must have spent a long time working on this paper.

Jennifer (age 7)
(Embarrassed)
I did it in fifteen minutes.

Teacher
You are good at writing, and fast, too. Excellent!

MORE RATIONAL
(objective)

Teacher
Do you enjoy writing stories?

Jennifer (age 7)
Yes.

Teacher
Is this one of your best or one of your longest?

Jennifer
It's one of my longest, but not one of my best.

Teacher
Which part of the story do you like best?

Jennifer
The middle part. I used my best writing there.

Teacher
Thank you for showing it to me.

13. Private Reprimanding

To reprimand a child privately is not the opposite of public praising. Here we want to preserve the child's dignity and we want to protect the rest of the class (sometimes more sensitive students) so that they are not alarmed by the reprimand. In some cases, private reprimanding serves the purpose of isolating an unpleasant form of behavior of one particular child and prevent it from spreading to other children.

Reprimanding should be factual and never degrading. The teacher should always look for the opportunity to congratulate the child for understanding the necessity of stopping unacceptable behavior and for cooperating.

VERBALIZATION EXAMPLE

LESS RATIONAL (as punishment, degrading)	MORE RATIONAL (positive, friendly)

LESS RATIONAL
(as punishment, degrading)

Teacher
Jane, come with me. I have something to say to you.

I have seen you put the cube of the pink tower in your lunch box. I will not put up with this. If I see you take small pieces of materials home with you, I will call your parents and see that they get you to stop. Do you understand?

Jane (age 3)
(frightened and humilated)
Yes.

MORE RATIONAL
(positive, friendly)

Teacher
Jane, would you please come with me? I have something to say to you.

I think you'd really like to have the small cube of the pink tower, don't you?

Jane (age 3)
Yes.

Teacher
Well, I am so glad to know that you like this piece of material. I wish we had one set for each child in the class, but we only have one to share. If you take this one away we won't have any at all. Do you think you can put the small cube back all by yourself?

Jane
Yes.

Teacher
I'm so glad you had it, and it didn't get lost forever. What would we do if someone took it home and never brought it back? None of the children could use the pink tower, would they? Thank you for keeping it with you and putting it back.

14. Written Agreement

A technique suitable for older children, this approach is designed to apply the concept of cooperation for mutual benefit. When two conflicting values exist between the adult and the child, it is worthwhile to point out in writing what each is willing to do for the other. Children who often verbally promise to do their part, frequently default on their verbal promises and learn to take full advantage of the inconsistency of adults.

Adults are often distracted, divided in their various pursuits. They themselves promise to follow through with their responsibilities or their intentions, but much against their will, often remember all too late what they were supposed to do for or with someone else.

Children, too, learn to behave inconsistently, either by being honestly absent-minded or by pure manipulation. The technique of the written agreement is beneficial for breaking strongly established patterns of inconsistencies both in adults and children.

VERBALIZATION EXAMPLE

LESS RATIONAL
(without written agreement)

Adult
You have been promising me that you would complete this math work in one day. The last time I spoke to you about it was more than a week ago.

Child (age 9)
I know. I have been trying to do it, but every time something else would come up. I promise that I'll do this work next.

(Three days later the math work was still left unfinished.)

MORE RATIONAL
(with written agreement)

Adult
You have been promising me that you would complete this work in one day. This was last week.

Child (age 9)
I know. I promise I'll do it next.

Adult
And if you don't? Let's write an agreement for each other to remind us both. What can you really accomplish in the next half hour? Can you do three problems.

Child
Yes.

Adult
Good. Let's write down an agreeable schedule to get it all done.

15. Re-Directing

In the event that a child is unfocused or scattered in his/her attention, the technique of re-directing is useful. This technique is also necessary in case the child is too focused, too fixed upon a destructive or conflicting activity. This is particularly true with small preschool children.

A teacher often has the occasion of having to re-direct a child's attention towards the activities of the classroom and away from say, the child's mother. A small child may go through a short period of transition when separating from mother and the home environment.

The technique of re-directing (or distracting the child's attention) is of paramount importance in this case. A child cannot hold in the brain simultaneously two opposite feelings. You cannot be happy and unhappy at the same time. You cannot be angry and joyful at the same time.

If a small child's emotions are fixed on separating from the mother, he may be crying. We must then bring into play something that captures the child's attention dramatically. If the teacher can find some interesting, stimulating activity with an element of surprise, the child stops focusing on the mother and for a moment his attention is diverted to something else. If the new stimulus is indeed of interest to the child, it is quite easy to lead the child on to completely different thoughts and for the child to easily forget his mother.

VERBALIZATION EXAMPLE

LESS RATIONAL (intellectualizing)	MORE RATIONAL (new stimulus)

LESS RATIONAL

(intellectualizing)

Child (age 3) (crying)
I want my mommy!

Teacher
Mommy has to go home now, but we can do some nice games.

Child (screaming)
No! I don't want to do games. I want my mommy.

Teacher
But look at all the children working. They don't cry. They are happy with their work.

I have many things I want to show you.

Child
No! I want my mommy!

MORE RATIONAL

(new stimulus)

Child (age 3) (crying)
I want my mommy!

Teacher
Yes, I'll call your mommy, if you stop crying.

Child (sobbing)
OK.

Teacher
First I want to see if we can find the baby rabbits in the bushes. (Teacher picks up the child in her arms and points at some bushes.) I think I saw the rabbits hiding in there. Do you see them?

Child (now attentively looking into the bushes)
I saw something moving.

Teacher
Is that a rabbit or a raccoon?

Child
It's a birdy!

Teacher and child enjoy a few minutes of fun interaction. The child is calmer, more ready to reason, not fixed on mother.

Teacher
Let's go see what the children are doing in the classroom. After I show you a game I'll go to the office and call your mother and tell her to come pick you up very soon, OK?

Child
OK.

16. Stating Expectations

The ability of the teacher to state clear expectations, either of the class as a whole or of the individual children, is valuable for effective communication and class normalization.

Many teachers lack clear expectations. It is not sufficient to ask that the class behave, or that one child sit properly.

The terms "behave" and "properly" do not describe to the children any specific expectation. The child is not guided to success by the use of general directions, on the contrary, he/she is being set up for sure failure.

The idea of stating expectations is similar to the idea of giving accurate presentations in the use of the Montessori materials. Similarly, we can expect the same precision in the way we want children to conduct themselves.

VERBALIZATION EXAMPLE

LESS RATIONAL
(vague expectations)

Teacher
It's time to clean up the classroom. I would like to see the children put away their materials properly on the shelves and be ready for serving a snack.

MORE RATIONAL
(descriptive expectations)

Teacher
When the bell rings, I expect to see everyone frozen and turned towards me. I am not going to make the announcement until I see everyone still and until I hear no noise at all from within the classroom.

Now, I'll call one person to put away his or her materials. We are going to watch how quietly the materials are put away. I am going to watch if they are put away straight on the shelves or sloppily; if the rugs are rolled up carefully; if the mats are neatly rearranged. I'll watch for those children who sit down, ready to be called, and how well they'll wait while the others finish clearing their work.

17. Relating Values

The essence of this technique lies in the ability to expose the fact that at times teacher and child may have different values in mind, especially when the values are the source of conflict between child and adult. Once the teacher has been able to identify the child's values, without accepting them or without condemning them, a dialogue is possible. Such a dialogue is intended to reach mutual understanding and often an exchange of values. The technique simply works as a trade: You do your part for my sake and I'll do my part for your sake. Both of us get what we want at a fair price and neither one loses.

To expose different values, the teacher must be able to penetrate the child's mind, be a keen observer of the child's motives, desires and interests. If, as an adult, you would like the child to come to read to you, for example, and the child refuses, or consistently shuns that activity, you must be able to come in contact with the truth of the relationship. A teacher wants the child to learn, practice and appreciate reading *(our value)* while the child, for an indefinite number of reasons, does not.

Should we not find out what could possibly be the child's value at this time? What would the child choose to do instead of reading? I could guess a number of possibilities, but a sure way to find out is to ask the child himself, with respect, without a shade of threat, without contempt or intimidation.

VERBALIZATION EXAMPLE

LESS RATIONAL	MORE RATIONAL
(without relating values)	(relating values)

LESS RATIONAL (without relating values)

Child (age 6)
I don't want to read.

Adult
Reading is very important. How will you be able to know what people write in books, and magazines when you grow up if you do not learn to read?

Child
I don't care about what people write in books and magazines.

Adult
But all the children come to school to learn to read. That's why your parents send you to school. Are you too tired today?

Child
Yes, I am too tired.

Adult
Shall we read tomorrow?

Child
Yes.

MORE RATIONAL (relating values)

Child (age 6)
I don't want to read.

Adult
Reading is no fun for you, is it?

Child
I hate reading!

Adult
Of all the activities in the school, which one do you really like best?

Child
I like to paint.

Adult
Do you do a lot of painting?

Child
I paint every day at school and at home. I love making paintings of rockets.

Adult
When did you read last?

Child
I don't know.

Adult
Three days ago we read a whole page together. Then you became very tired. Can you read just this much (about the same as last time) with me everyday and then do a painting?

Child
Yes.

The technique of relating values starts with the concept that one must name the reality of the relationship. The child's actual feeling: "You really would love to spend your time painting, don't you?" Then the reality of the adult: "I really would like for you to read with me every day, that is what I am here for, but you really would like to paint. Is there anything that we can do to please each other?"

This type of relationship is unique. It is a moment in which both child and adult are real, visible to each other. How are we going to put different values together? Both have to cooperate in order to gain something out of each other. This is possible without using force, power, repression or intimidation.

Relating values, as a technique, can encourage the child to want to manipulate the adult. Interns and inexperienced teachers may easily fall in the verbal maze. They may end up spending hours discussing in great details the value of a child drawing pictures versus the value of the adult wishing the child did his academic work. One must consider what values are exchangeable.

A student who is severely deviated holds severely deviated values. Deviated values cannot really be exchanged. You cannot condone violent behavior, destructive, insulting or disrespectful behavior and consider that a legitimate value of the child to be exchanged. You cannot say: "Your value is to be disrespectful to me. I'll let you be disrespectful in exchange for reading." A thief has values, but these values are irrational, deviated and non-relatable. You cannot relate with force, power or violence. Relationship is possible only through respect and only rational values are worthy of admiration and respect.

QUESTION AND ANSWER DIALOGUE

Student Teacher:

What if a child does not value anything? Shouldn't honesty be the ultimate value to be established between the child and the adult so that the child is brought up in harmony with the adult?

Mr. A.:

At times it is difficult to identify the child's values. But children inevitably do have values. Values can be permanent or they can be created for temporary use and then substituted. Values are personal issues. We acquire and dismiss them all the time. What we valued once, we may not continue to value at present.

Honesty is not a value. Honesty and integrity in relationship are prerequisites for understanding and for relating with another. Values are personal and can be chosen. We cannot choose honesty any more than we can choose intelligence. We cannot say today I'll choose to be honest, rational and intelligent while tomorrow I might not. Without honesty valuable relationships are not possible.

Let's say I have a deviation. By observing and acknowledging my deviation, I can learn about it. By denying a deviation, I simply prevent myself from relating. The deviation does not go away by denial. I must study and check my premises, observe my hierarchy of values and restructure it so that my thinking adheres to reality, instead of contradicting it.

18. Withholding Privileges

This technique is often used in conjunction with the previous one (Relating Values). The teacher can use this technique only if the relationship between the child and the adult is clearly set: the child respects the teacher as the adult, and the teacher respects the child as the student.

Just as it is appropriate for the student to look up to the teacher for guidance and with admiration, so it is important that the adult regard the child with enjoyment, affection, and with a sincere desire to achieve success.

The responsibilities of the adult are not equal to the responsibilities of the child. It is this natural inequality that bestows privileges to the adult that are not open to the child. The technique of withholding privileges works on the basis of this disparity between child and adult. On the other hand, where the adult is indistinguishably equal to the child, this technique does not apply because guidance is not possible.

A relationship of "equality" is not necessarily a correct relationship. Two blind men do not provide any better vision for each other. Similarly, two children cannot raise each other effectively.

The concept of having a privilege is delicate. On one hand, we see the necessity for the child to arrive at independence and achieve the ability of making one's own decisions; on the other, we are keenly aware of the child's limited amount of knowledge and experience.

It is clear to a parent and a teacher that the role of the adult is to guide the child towards independence gradually. Guidance, by its nature, implies allowance, freedom within certain limits, the limits of rationality.

Can one teach a child the concept of property and at the same time withhold a privilege? What is the difference between a privilege and a right? Are the child's toys, for example, the child's rightful property? Or, is the child merely enjoying the privilege of *using* toys which were bought by the adult?

To resolve this problem — one that all parents and teachers must confront — we must hold firmly in mind the distinguishing characteristics between the child and the adult. The distinguishing characteristic is not the physical size, not age, not even knowledge and experience, but the degree of responsibility. This single aspect clearly marks the borderline between the child and the adult.

Holding property involves a different kind of responsibility from the concept of mere possession. In general, children possess objects rather than own them. In the process of educating children, most adults do not distinguish ownership from possession. Such distinction of concepts is not usually brought to the child's awareness in daily living. Thus a great deal of confusion is absorbed subconsciously. As adults are ambiguous between rights and privileges, property and possession, children often grow up unaware of what it means to earn and own property.

It is from understanding and applying these concepts correctly that parents and teachers may establish trustworthy, respectful relationships with children. All too often these concepts have been distorted, twisted or even plainly ignored to the point of severe tension and conflict in relationship. All children must grow up to judge the trustworthiness of their parents and their teachers. When that moment comes, will it be admiration or resentment that the adults had sown?

VERBALIZATION EXAMPLE

LESS RATIONAL
(confusing rights/privileges)

Adult
I noticed that you leave your toys out for me to put away.

Child (age 7)
You don't have to put them away. I like my room the way it is and those are *my* toys, anyway.

Adult
But sometimes we have to clean and vacuum it and it is impossible to do that with all this clutter.

Child (righteously)
You can clean it another time. Why now? It isn't that dirty, anyway. Can't I have *my* room the way I want it?

Adult (with impatience)
I am tired of arguing. I want this room cleaned up. Put your toys away right now!

MORE RATIONAL
(distinguishing a right from a privilege)

Adult
I noticed that you leave your toys out for me to put away.

Child (age 7)
Why can't I have *my* toys and *my* room how I wish?

Adult
These toys and this room are for you to use, but *I* decide how it should be kept. Which do you prefer: for me to pick up the toys and keep them for you, or for you to pick them up and keep them in the room always available? I think if I keep them, it will be easier for you. You can ask for a few at a time and we'll agree to put them away beforehand.

Child
No. I think I prefer to put them away now and keep them in the room.

Adult
That's an excellent decision. Remind me to talk to you some day about the difference between a privilege and a right and the difference between possession and ownership.

Child
OK.

I
Fostering Intelligence and Rationality
As the Main Role of the Teacher

Although intelligence can be defined as the capacity to acquire knowledge and apply it, neuroscientists themselves have difficulty isolating the essential components of such a capacity. In daily living, the analysis and meticulous study performed by scientists will probably affect us very little. Much of what is being observed and discovered in the study of how the human brain functions has immense value in the scientific community for the development of effective medicines, appropriate surgical procedures or psychiatric work aimed at curing diseases or correcting mental aberrations.

In the course of conducting normal, every day business, people must rely primarily on their *rational judgment* for their competence at living. Thus, education, not neurosurgery or psychiatry, is the normal sphere of knowledge in which the mind of all individuals must operate.

In educating the human potential, surely intelligence cannot be separated from rationality. It is with this understanding that we shall speak of intelligence here. The manner in which judgment is applied (rational or irrational) is therefore the realm of our observation in educating the human potential.

Intelligence Quotient (IQ), for example, although important in determining environmental and curricular placement of a student, is not the main aspect of our discussion. Here, we are not learning to become experts in administering IQ tests, for instance, but our minds must be prepared to be engaged at observing *how* individual students learn, because every human being, child and adult, is confronted with the same common denominator: the necessity to deal with life's challenges effectively. If the essential goal of education is to meet this common, universal need of mankind, then the role of the teacher is not different from the role of a scientist and the teacher must be inspired, like the scientist, by one's own love for truth, nature and the facts of reality.

We can think of intelligence as the ability to meet life's challenges rationally, effectively. This means, also, that an intelligent human being is aware of what lies beyond his skills, his capabilities and, respectful of reality, such a person would not attempt a task without acquiring the necessary preparation.

A teacher who is not just an instructor of a specific academic subject, but a guide to efficient living, is an individual who sets out, like a scientist, to investigate and observe what laws or principles govern human relationship in general. By studying and understanding such principles, the Montessori Guide acquires what Dr. Montessori called the "spiritual training" that prepares us appropriately for a rational approach in education. This spiritual preparation, Dr. Montessori felt, is so essential, she considered it the main feature distinguishing the Montessori Guide from the conventionally trained teacher.

Often, in her books and lectures, Dr. Montessori impressed on her audiences semi-mystical descriptions of the universal principles we must study in order to acquire the spiritual training for a new, rational education. Such descriptions were designed, in agreement with Montessori's own spiritual tendencies, to bridge the gap between the scientist, the lover of truth and the dreamer, the believer within us all.

Effective and charismatic as she was, people felt touched by words that described precisely their own experiences and problems with traditional education. Many of us were inspired by certain analogies, certain passionate correlations and, perhaps for the first time, clearly saw the terrible damaging effects of the traditional system and the necessity of replacing it with a scientific method to educate the human potential.

Regardless of how Dr. Montessori chose to express the principles of rational education, the student of her method will find that all laws and principles governing human relationship can be stated in simple terms and must be corroborated by the facts of reality, by nature, by the laws of life itself. Repeatedly, Dr. Montessori prompted her students not to take her words dogmatically, but rather to verify the truth of a principle through direct experience and scientific observation.

The moral preparation of a teacher in Montessori education must be undoubtedly founded on the commitment that the teacher has made in removing all obstacles that impede the development of intelligence and rationality in children. The Montessori Guide's highest goal must be to see that students are provided with the conditions suitable for achieving competence at living.

Truthfully, the teacher is the living model in the business of education. Only those of us who have made it a commitment to develop our own intelligence and rationality may hope to help students develop theirs. This sense of complete concern for one's own well-being and personal achievement is a theme that Dr. Montessori often used in describing the universal law of self-achievement in harmony with nature and the rest of life.

Biology provides countless examples of this principle when we observe how different organisms within an ecosystem are inter-related. While each type of organism performs its function strictly for its own sake and survival, a higher task is being achieved, a task of harmony and integration with the rest of life. Similarly, in the education of children, it is precisely by functioning as rational, loving adults for our personal achievement at living competently that we can hope to truly inspire the children to do the same.

It is this type of reward that the Montessori Guide aspires to obtain: the intrinsic pleasure derived by learning and discovering the magnitude and beauty of nature by meeting the challenges of life.

When we ask the question: "How do we foster intelligence in children?" We should rephrase the question to read: "How do I foster intelligence in myself?" In this manner, the teacher and the pupil become embodied in the same person in a non-contradictory way. The teacher's lessons will not be different from the teacher's discoveries, and only then will the teacher be prepared to offer guidance to the pupil.

The adult who wishes to be a Montessori Guide must possess the quality of the ardent fire of intelligence — never ceasing to burn, always seeking to maintain the flame of rationality alive. For this person, the highest value is the triumph of intelligent living. It is not sufficient for the scientist to be content with repeating the same experiment.

As soon as a challenge of life has been adequately met, the flame of intelligence naturally seeks the next challenge. Similarly, the Montessori Guide uses the classroom and observes accurate, scientific procedures to see that successful results are taking place. Each child is a challenge of his own, each lesson must be presented with great care, the classroom must be prepared to afford independence, respect and joy of learning.

With this spiritual preparation, the role of the new teacher is of the utmost importance in fostering intelligence and rationality. Since the adult uses education to develop intelligence and rationality in the children, it becomes obvious that the person interested in becoming a Montessori Guide must consciously assume a great deal of responsibility. Although the mental potential of each child varies considerably -- some children have a high memory retention while others seem to lack it, some children mature emotionally sooner than others -- the intelligence, sensitivity and preparation of the teacher represent the factors capable of making the difference between success or failure for all types of children.

At variance with the traditional classroom, the teacher in a Montessori environment establishes a personal working relationship with each individual student. Each relationship is different, but the Montessori Guide knows that the flame of intelligence in each student must receive adequate attention in order to ensure its growth and natural development.

Never losing sight of the highest purpose of education, the teacher seeks to guide each student, no matter how different, towards the satisfaction of an identical and universally common need: the need to build one's competence at living through rationality. No lesson is more important than the satisfaction of this need, no academic subject should take priority over this fundamental purpose of education.

Once we have established that the highest priority of education is not merely the instruction of academic subjects, but the development of intelligence, it is logical to ask ourselves what method we should employ in such a process and how one can take such a responsibility.

The means by which academic subjects are ordinarily acquired rely primarily on memorization and repetition through practicing. Are these means also applicable to the development of intelligence and rationality? What other tools are at our disposal to achieve this task?

As we observe how our own brain functions, undoubtedly we'll come to distinguish two main processes. The brain employs the *cognitive process* when acquiring knowledge of facts. In this process, memory retention plays the most important role. The brain also is designed to make value judgments. We call this the *appraisal process.*

The cognitive process is used when a child must understand the difference between the quantities represented by the numeral 1 and the numeral 10, for example, or the difference between a mammal and an amphibian, or between a noun and a verb, or between a living and a non-living entity. The appraisal process is used when a student must decide if shaking the table is as appropriate as smiling to a friend; if playing a prank on someone is going to be received as a gesture of friendship or an inimical, insulting act; if being disruptive is the same as being funny and popular. The appraisal process of the brain implies making an appropriate judgment in accordance with the circumstances.

While the cognitive process depends largely on the accumulation of knowledge, the appraisal process depends more on the kinds of abstractions we arrive at. Contradictory, irrational abstractions necessarily influence negatively the appraisal process. In turn, from poor appraisal poor behavior ensues.

The old concept of education and of teacher deals primarily with imparting knowledge and transmitting information, often with no regard to the maturity of the students, without considering their genuine interests or their personal commitment. The Montessori method insists on the idea that the integrity of the individual is more important than practicing and memorizing answers compelled by punishments or rewards in order to pass tests. In this approach, the appraisal process is given precedence over the cognitive process.

It will be important that both the teacher and the student know *why* something ought to be studied before deciding what method to use, when to apply it and what effort is needed. With very small children, it will be important that curiosity and joy of learning, not entertainment, be the motives for coming to school. A small child who is not ready to leave the comfort and security of the home should stay at home.

To teach students how to evaluate relationships and make appropriate judgments is much more difficult than to teach them the academic subjects. Precisely because happiness and creativity depend essentially on the ability to make correct decisions, the Montessori Guide must be first concerned with developing the process of appraisal in a systematic way.

If rationality is the standard or the prerequisite for a happy and efficient life, how can we be sure that our abstractions are rational? And how can we distinguish the rational from the irrational abstractions within our mind?

The teacher must learn the techniques that help him root out contradictions. Only in this manner can we be certain that what is being held by thought is in agreement with reality, therefore rational. As we learn to root out our own contradictions, we teach children how to root out theirs.

A teacher is usually sensitive to the children's lack of knowledge and, almost naturally, he or she tries to fill in the gaps of academic learning by providing stimulating or interesting anecdotes, activities, books or materials for the purpose. The same sensitivity and commitment are often absent when it comes to bridging the gaps of learning rational judgment and emotional maturity. In this field, the adult is often as confused as the child, utterly incompetent, and the child is left to his own resources, compelled to learn from concrete, painful experiences that frequently leave the individual traumatized.

VERBALIZATION EXAMPLE

The Montessori classroom is a small community of children and adults working together. As in all communities, the need for rules arises strictly from the violation of individual rights or, more specifically, from arbitrary restrictions on personal liberty. A student harassing another, for instance, violates the basic liberty of someone.

What rational rule should the Montessori teachers invoke if such a case should arise? If punishment and authority are not rational means for developing competent appraisal, what techniques ought to be applied? And if leaving the students to their own resources prompts an escalation of the problem, instead of mutual respect and understanding, what alternatives are open to us?

By studying the principles of rational relationship, we ought to select the appropriate techniques and resolve seemingly puzzling peer disputes like the following.

LESS RATIONAL (children must learn to solve their own problems—somehow)	MORE RATIONAL (children are guided and shown how some specific principles and techniques produce respect and mutual cooperation)
Richard (age 8) Charles takes my work and hides it from me. He tells jokes about me and makes everyone laugh.	*Richard* (age 8) Charles takes my work and hides it from me. He tells jokes about me and makes everyone laugh.
Teacher Surely you and Charles can work this problem out together. You are even older than he is. Go ahead. Talk to him. I'll make sure that he listens to you. I want to see you guys learn to get along as friends in my classroom.	*Teacher* It sounds like Charles is imposing on you and annoying you. We both need to talk to him. Ask him to come and see me.
(Richard and Charles talk it over. Charles is aware of the teacher's expectations and acts apologetic and cooperative only to start tormenting Richard a few minutes later with a different kind of disturbance.)	*Charles* (age 9) I was just having fun. His papers are right there.
	Teacher Do you think that Richard is having as much fun as you?

65

Charles
No. But . . . he doesn't have to be
that serious about it.

Richard
It bothers me to find my papers
disappear and it bothers me when
they laugh behind my back.

Teacher
Is it right to have fun at the expense of another person? Do you
enjoy seeing Richard upset?

Charles
No. But it is funny.

Teacher
What if three or four children had
fun at your expense, teased you
and laughed about your feelings,
do you think it would be alright?

Charles
No.

Teacher
Do you have a suggestion to solve
this problem?

Charles
I'll stop. I'm sorry, Richard.

II
Independence and Good Judgment: Two Essential Ingredients of Happiness and Success

Independence, like the idea of freedom, can be easily misunderstood. There is, of course, such a thing as independence from something or from the oppression of someone. The need for the basic necessities of living (food, shelter, clothing, etc.) must be met, or independence is affected by serious physical discomforts. Freedom of movement, for instance, can be severely curtailed by stringent authoritarian governments, thus, our physical freedom and independence is diminished. These are examples where independence is *physically* restricted by blatant coercion imposed by circumstances beyond human control or by the abuse of powerful people over others.

Physically, independence simply means the freedom, opportunity and ability to provide for our basic needs of survival. Such level of independence is achieved through scientific and technological progress as well as through the establishment of a society or civilization where the rights of the individual are respected, where justice prevails and power is never abused.

For the educator, however, the proper subject of our study is not physical independence, but *psychological* independence. We could define psychological independence as the specific process of thinking from which the healthy individual discovers how values are correctly aligned in agreement with reality. The search for more technical advances, the accumulation of wealth and material possessions, though physically beneficial, do not automatically bestow more psychological independence.

Unfortunately, the traditional method has required that the teacher be prepared in the academic subjects and be familiar with child development education from the old concepts of thinking, but it has neglected the spiritual preparation of a

67

rational approach. The Montessori Guide, therefore, will pay much attention to the idea of developing psychological independence both for oneself and for the students. Psychological independence is, in fact, the natural consequence of a type of spiritual education based on thinking rationally, non-contradictorily.

Psychological independence is necessary for every human being's sanity. For a person to be self-directed, independent, there must be a clear understanding of the essence of maturity.

It is valid to ask oneself the question: "Is independence the product of readiness for the next level of learning, for meeting the next challenge?" In Montessori education we prepare the environment and the curriculum to meet the readiness and needs of the children. In traditional education the lessons, the curriculum and environment do not provide any allowance for the child's individual capabilities, for his needs or previous preparation.

What regulates the process of psychological independence or maturity? Inevitably, the answer to this question is the pleasure/pain mechanism. Pleasure and pain (particularly at the psychological level) are perceived differently by people. Through personal experiences, education and culture, we arrive at the formation of different abstractions and different values. The hierarchic scale of values varies tremendously from person to person. What is desirable for one person may be of insignificant value to another. It is the abstractions we have made about something in relation to pleasure and pain, it is that which we learned to value that motivates us towards dependence or independence, maturity or immaturity. Fundamentally, at the root of each value, at the root of each abstraction lies the same universal standard of judgment: the pleasure/pain mechanism.

Knowing this principle is extremely helpful in education; it allows us to reduce quickly all complex activities, motivations, emotions and forms of behavior to one basic universally inescapable movement: the search for pleasure and the desire to escape pain. At the root of all intentions, of all human behavior one will inexorably find this motive.

Keeping this principle in mind, what could possibly be the reason for a child to maintain a dependent or immature behavior? The answer is very easy: a child remains dependent or immature as long as he or she has abstracted that dependence and immaturity pay off. The task of the teacher is to see that the child's abstractions are corrected. The task of the teacher is also to see that the child clearly understand that dependence and immaturity *never* pay off. In the long run, they can never lead to pleasure.

Is there a concept of independence that does not have anything to do with context? Surely we cannot say that we are mature because we can drive a car. The object is not what determines psychological maturity or independence. In every context there must be the essence of independence. Once we discover the essence of independence, then we can help the child move from dependence to independence by following rational principles.

In particular, I am thinking about what the motivating force to be independent is, where it comes from. Is independence something I can desire, is it something that I must want? Was I educated to want it? Unless we discover this, we cannot pass on to the children the principles of maturity and independence they so desperately need.

Surely independence is self-reliance, and self-reliance is the very essence of individuality, living integrally. One has no choice about it. The nature of man is to be self-reliant, both physically and psychologically.

By understanding that to be responsible (*response-able*) we really mean to be capable of responding correctly to the challenges of life, we can truly understand that the ultimate state of independence is a state of conscious responsibility. Like any other learned skill, responsibility must be elicited by the teacher. If the child's education has neglected reason as the basic tool in developing responsibility, the child will remain emotionally immature. His self-esteem will suffer and his ability to respond correctly to the challenges of life will remain severely hampered. All this will inevitably have a tragic effect on his psychological and, ultimately, physical freedom. What are the principles that bring about a *response-able* person?

The essential charactistics of independence are maturity and responsibility — the capability of responding rationally and with maturity to the challenges of life. There are degrees of independence and maturity, of course. You adhere to independence to the degree that you adhere to maturity and rationality. When a child comes to school and is being disruptive, is the child dependent or independent? Obviously the child is not independent.

Independence implies no contradiction with rationality. A definition, a concept of independence divorced from rationality is invalid, because it would not adhere to reality. When you see a child who acts like an adult, prematurely, you often say that this child is independent. But often such a child is confronted prematurely with adult problems and forced by unusual conditions to act beyond his preparation.

One way of measuring someone's level of independence according to objective standards is to observe how rationally one acts. Actions that are not in contradiction with the environment are actions ensuing from independent individuals. We as teachers have to be prepared to understand these concepts so that we may be well equipped to help create the correct environment that fosters independence.

It is necessary to apply pedagogical techniques by using our judgment according to context. Obviously, it is our understanding of the principles of rationality that will guide and dictate our choice and use of the correct techniques.

A child who derives a great pleasure from working with the teacher all the time will have associated that the teacher (not the work) is his source of pleasure. When the teacher leaves to help another child, that child will act immature, will stop working, will be dependent.

How does a teacher correctly help this kind of child become more psychologically independent, what is the procedure? In these cases, of course, the procedure varies from context to context. The blend of techniques also varies in each situation, but the guiding principles will remain consistently the same.

To foster psychological independence we must always ask ourselves: What does this child have to gain in becoming independent? How can this child become conscious of the value of independence? How is he going to come to it? What help can I offer that would bring the child to value independence? These are the questions one must hold in mind while offering oneself as a guide to the child.

Dr. Montessori would ask us to be keen observers of the child's inner motives. What is the motivation of the child who is enjoying the company of the teacher? The child has identified that the teacher is his source of pleasure and Dr. Montessori's observation would probably be like this: Why do I say that this child is dependent? I could answer in two ways:

a) I find it annoying that this child needs me so frequently. The more I encourage independent work, the more this child seems to need my attention.
b) I think it is necessary for this child to be with me as frequently as possible in order to accomplish anything productive. It seems like productive work can only occur if I give exclusive attention to him.

Our awareness of these reasons is of paramount importance in the process of teaching and leading the child to independence.

We would have to question whether the child's independence is in any way related to enhancing our own satisfaction and pleasure, or if by keeping the child dependent we may not be allowing the child higher pleasure. If we are the cause that denies the child higher pleasure, what is our real role as teachers?

We all agree that independence is our goal. We don't differ in the goals. We differ in the understanding of the principles that govern a relationship based on independence.

What are the factors of such a relationship? The child is seeking pleasure and I am seeking pleasure. Don't the two movements, the two motives contradict each other? It always seems as though if the child is having his pleasure, it's at our expense. If we are having our way, the child's perceives it as being at his expense. That's what contradiction is, isn't it?

Is there a non-contradictory way of looking at the question of pleasure? The correct application of the pleasure/pain principle provides us with the opportunity to determine which technique and which verbalization is most suitable to ensure a child/adult relationship based on independence.

VERBALIZATION EXAMPLE

The child shows psychological dependence by demanding that the teacher stay with him when doing some work. The child stops working when the teacher leaves to give a lesson to another child.

LESS RATIONAL

Teacher
Why do you stop working when I leave? I just showed you how to do that work. Can't you go back and do it by yourself?

Child (age 5)
(whining)
I don't remember how.

Teacher
Yes you do! I just showed you. You know I have other children with whom I need to work. You must be independent.

Child (still whining)
I don't like this work anymore.

MORE RATIONAL

Teacher
Have you already finished the exercise you started with me?

Child (age 5)
I forgot how to do it.

Teacher
Would you like for me to come and see it?

Child
Yes.

Teacher
First I would like you to stay here with me and watch this lesson I'm giving this other child. Then I'll come back to your table.

Teacher (later)
Let's go and see your work. I see you do remember how to do it. I bet you won't be able to do it by yourself, though. I think you really like for me to watch you do it, don't you?

Child
Yes.

Teacher
Let's make an agreement. I'll come and watch you for a while,

72

and you do the work by yourself for a while. When you do this much, come and tell me and I'll come back and watch you work some more. OK?

Child
OK.

III
Establishing Child/Adult Respect

Knowing that each person has a built-in concept of respect, is there a way to find a common denominator? What are the essential characteristics that identify what we mean by respect?

Although the dictionary definition of a word is necessary for superficial communication, when it comes to applying a concept such as respect to relationship, the dictionary definition falls short of real meaning.

The concept of respect that we actually use in relationship will necessarily be the one we already have built in ourselves at the emotional level, certainly not the abstract definition of the dictionary. Therefore, it is important to know what conditioned concepts of respect we already have.

We must know our personal concept of what respect means to us, according to the standards we have been given by our parents, by our teachers and by the society in which we were brought up as children. We can only come to an objective and valid concept of respect after we have understood and discarded the conditioned, irrational concepts of respect we acquired subconsciously.

Objectivity becomes possible only after we expose, understand and dispassionately discard our subjective views as being invalid. In order to arrive at an objective concept of respect, we must study our prejudices and observe closely the contradictions in our personal, subjective concepts of respect. This kind of ruthless inquiry will permit us to integrate respect in our everyday life and consequently in the life of the children we educate.

Respect in relationship can be the response of predetermined, mostly subconscious, feelings we acquired as children. As a fact of rational living, it has no validity. It is merely a learned behavioral pattern. The recitations and ritualistic statements we make with redundancy every day when we meet someone, are often part of cultural habits, with very little to do with respect.

For respect to be valid, it must contain the essence of *rational relationship*. It must stem from the understanding that efficient living is possible only if human relationships are non-contradictory, devoid of conflict.

Respect must take into consideration context and the type of relationship one is creating or the type of relationship one is responding to. If the goal is always a non-contradictory relationship, then respect is always based on rational standards and not on precepts learned without validation.

VERBALIZATION EXAMPLE #1

LESS RATIONAL	MORE RATIONAL
The concept of respect is categorical, prescriptive and disconnected from context.	The concept of respect is integrated with the concept of rational relationship.
Child (age 4) I want some juice.	*Child* (age 4) I want some juice.
Adult What kind of manners are those? Don't you know how to ask with respect?	*Adult* Do you know how to ask politely?
Child I don't know. I just asked for some juice.	*Child* I don't understand.
Adult I think that is very rude. Let me tell you how polite people ask. To be rude is to be disrespectful and you must always be respectful to me.	*Adult* It is respectful to ask like this: "May I have some juice, please?" *Child* Oh!

VERBALIZATION EXAMPLE #2

LESS RATIONAL

Respect is not an end in itself. One's self-esteem depends on how one is respected.
Respect is a status symbol, a personal image with no substance.

Child (age 6)
I don't like you!

Adult
What? Is that the way to talk to an adult? I told you it is not possible for you to have a friend over today.

Child
Yes.

Adult
What's the matter with you? Today is not a good day, that's all. Your toys are scattered all around and your room is a mess. First I want to see you straighten everything. I am not letting you have friends over to make an even bigger mess than this one.

Child
I hate you!

Adult
Apologize immediately. Do you hear? You have better learn some manners before you get some favors from me!

MORE RATIONAL

Respect is an end in itself, a personal achievement. Respect is a prerequisite for deeper and rational relationships.

Child (age 6)
I don't like you!

Adult
Have I done something to disturb you?

Child
Yes.

Adult
You would really be happy if each time you ask me for something, I'd say you can, wouldn't you?

Child
Well . . . yes.

Adult
I would love to be able to give you as many privileges as possible. I take care of the house and I have many responsibilities. Maybe I can do something special for you some day and you can do something special for me in exchange. How does that look to you?

Child
You mean I can have my friend over today?

Adult
First, can we agree to help each other and then plan for a suitable day to have your friend over?

76

Let's write down what you will
do for me and what I will do for
you in exchange, that way we can
both get what we want, alright?

Child
OK.

VERBALIZATION EXAMPLE #3

LESS RATIONAL

Fear is used to intimidate in order
to force respect. One's personal
image is more important than the
happiness of the relationship. One
believes that the child could not
respect the adult without fearing
the adult's power.

Child (age 9)
I don't want to finish my work.

Adult
Sorry, young man. You do not
have a choice and this work is
important.

Child
I hate this work! I have always
hated it!

Adult
Do you want to grow up lazy?
I tell you, I don't want to hear
anymore from you, or else. Get
down to work before I end up
whipping your bottom!

MORE RATIONAL

Respect elicits admiration.
Fairness in relationship is the
result of holding rationality as the
basis for a happy relationship.

Child (age 9)
I don't want to finish my work.

Adult
You would prefer to stop your
work now and start playing,
wouldn't you?

Child
Yes. I hate this work!

Adult
This is an unpleasant job, I must
say. Wouldn't it be nice if no one
had any work like this to do, ever?

Child
It surely would be nice.

Adult
Sometimes I wish one had some
magic words one could say, and
there, the work gets done all by
itself. Do you know any such
words?

77

Child
Oh, that's silly!

Adult
Can we think of some way to get this work done fast and easy?

Child
How?

Adult
Well, we could take a break if we can agree that you will be mature enough to get back to work when the break is over. What do you think?

Child
I'll take a break for an hour, then I'll finish it.

Adult
Can we agree on a half-hour break?

Child
OK.

Adult
But how will you stand it when I call you in half an hour? Will you give me a hard time and act really immature or will you be prompt and respectful to me? I need assurance that you won't throw a temper tantrum and act spoiled.

Child
I'll take a short break and I promise to finish my work afterwards.

What is the essential characteristic of respect? One is respectful when one treats others the way one wishes to be treated. Is this kind of equality, therefore, the essence of respect? Is the basis of respect the fact that human beings are essentially equal? Does respect demand an equal level of intensity in relationship? In meeting the child at his level, either by lowering myself down to him or by providing the conditions for the child to elevate himself up to the level of the adult, it is possible to have a respectful relationship. The dignity, the integrity of two people must be at the same level in order for respect to take place.

I find it easier to understand the nature and implications of respect by approaching it negatively. Surely respect does not mean violating someone's property. It does not mean violating someone's dignity. To put it positively, respect means to give consideration to other people's rational values. It is necessary, therefore, that we understand those values, that we be attuned with others to share the meaning of respect.

In order to admire and to value something, or someone, it is necessary to understand their beneficial and non-contradictory implications. In this way, we come to realize that respect is necessarily connected with love, and that love is possible only where value and consideration is given.

In searching for the principles that govern a relationship based on respect, one comes inevitably to the problem of responsibility. Whose responsibility is it to establish a respectful relationship, mine or someone else's? To be responsible in conducting ourselves respectfully in all relationships is part of a great sense of awareness.

Among adults of different cultures, people put out a great deal of effort in trying to meet each other's expectations, values and needs. No matter how hard they try, however, there seems to be a constant cultural barrier to be overcome. Unexpectedly, there always seems to be a point of unawareness of the other and a lapse into one's own cultural habits or routines. This particular problem is worth investigating on its own merit. Here, suffice to say that clearly in the child/adult relationship the burden of major responsibility for maintaining a respectful relationship rests with the adult. The child has no tools to carry out such activity.

The first thing to observe in the relationship between child and adult is to notice how dissimilar the values are between the two. It is precisely this factor that puts a major strain on the respectful relationship.

In general, children do not have the same values as adults, in fact, their values are widely different and often unknown. In this regard, we can observe that adults and children are often so estranged that they may actually be mentally and emotionally invisible to each other.

This condition is disastrous for maintaining a respectful relationship. It is an unfortunate condition, in all similar to that encountered by different species of wild animals which fortuitously happen to cross each other's path in the wilderness: if overt antagonism does not break out, in the best of events, after a few snarls and growls, the animals just move away from each other in different directions without a care.

The conviction that it is possible to establish a respectful relationship with children despite the fact that we have different values is a typical mistake that adults are prone to making very frequently. Usually, the adult simply disregards the child's values and subtly or overtly imposes his values on the child. Children, more often than not, conform to adult values, even though they do not hold those values for themselves.

By trying to establish respect despite the fact that we do not have common values, we violate a basic principle of human relationship. Parents say: "You must go to school, it's important; you must follow this ritual, it's important." Thus the child, without understanding, without volition, is taught to conform, to follow the values of the parent through mere obedience—a far cry from a respectful relationship.

As teachers, our job is to bring about the emotional awareness of values both in the child and in the adult. Obviously, cultural values, like all subjective values, are not valid. To teach cultural or personal values, without regard to rationality, is to meet with friction and to breed antagonism. Only the pursuit of rational values can bring about non-violent, non-abusive and respectful human relationship. Irrational values, subtly or overtly, are always imposed. They have their roots in manipulation or in the abuse of power, thus they inevitably breed conflict and contradiction.

One of the major challenges of maintaining a respectful relationship is the way we respond to disrespect, particularly when the child is disrespectful to us. We immediately have the tendency to react and to give the child another lesson on manners and proper behavior. We do not dwell on the fact that we are emotionally reacting, that we are offended by the way the child treated us, and whether we have anything to understand by the fact that we actually were insulted, injured and hurt in our pride.

Why should we be hurt or insulted at all by a child? What is our role as educators? Is it to protect our pride against the injury of children, or is it to teach children what respect is, so that they may learn to relate intelligently?

Obviously, by reacting to an insult, the adult is not exactly conveying to the child the work of intelligence. In reacting to an insult, we teach children that it is appropriate to retort, to intimidate and repress someone's feelings in order to preserve our dignity. We also teach them that it is justified to be hypocritical.

Without observing objectively the mechanism of hurt, of how we react to an insult, we are unable to change our habitual and mechanical ways. But in the process of understanding why we get psychologically hurt lie the seeds of human intelligence. It is this commitment to developing human intelligence that a teacher must hold as one's highest goal, nothing else.

If we took the position that children, in general, may be offensive not so much out of malice, but out of unawareness, what then would be the rational response to an insult? Would it really be correct to respond with power to unawareness?

If a child were to order me around, with a bossy tone of voice, for example, is he doing it for the specific purpose of insulting me? Or has he learned that to be bossy is the normal way of relating? As an adult, what else could I do, other than just repress his bossiness by scolding him or reacting emotionally? Could I learn to take that insult for what it actually is (a pattern of behavior subconsciously learned) and not look at it as a personal insult? Could I then bypass my sense of pride and be so relaxed about it, so untouched by it, that I could laugh and joke and make a game out of that bossy behavior? What consequences would my response elicit?

What message would I pass on to the child if my response had no anger, no hostility and no sense of injury in it?

Another irrational concept of respect that we may be holding is when respect is viewed as a state of being, a point of achievement. Now that I have respect, I got it made. Respect, of course, is not a point of arrival. Respect is the prerequisite for a rational relationship and it must be maintained from moment to moment throughout one's life. It is never a static achievement that can be arrived at and acquired with a maintenance guarantee.

Respect is possible only if either the child comes up to the adult's values and learns to appreciate them or the adult understands the child's values and relates with the child at his level of values. A respectful relationship could not occur in any other way.

VERBALIZATION EXAMPLE #4

LESS RATIONAL	MORE RATIONAL
Child (age 8) I don't like you!	*Child* (age 8) I don't like you!
Teacher Why?	*Teacher* Oh my! That's terrible because I wanted to be your friend.
Child Because you always make me do all this school work that I don't like.	*Child* Well, I don't like all this work you make me do.
Teacher We come to school to learn and we must do our work. I am sorry that you don't like spelling and math, but we must do those things.	*Teacher* Oh well, that's better. It's the work you don't like, but you do like me a little, don't you?
	Child Yes.
	Teacher Shall we talk about the work? Would you like to take a break from it?
	Child Yes.

Still another irrational concept of respect is when one believes that respect is the outcome of some sort of fear of authority. Using fear and authority to induce respect is all too common a part of the traditional system. Yet, factually, we know that no amount of fear or authority can bring about true respect. Admiration (which is the true meaning of respect) can never be brought about through fear of authority.

Authority, with its sense of fear — be it the fear of losing one's pride, one's dignity, or the fear of losing one's image of being powerful, successful, intelligent, knowledgeable, etc. — actually perpetuates fear. It teaches children that through power one can conquer psychological insecurity. In fact, authoritarian power invites conflict. When the child refuses to conform to the authority, the child rebels.

Rebelliousness, like authority, are reactions to each other. Neither one is part of respect, but they both are conducted in the name of respect.

Authority is legitimated in the name of respect, and rebellion also demands legitimacy in the name of respect. Neither one uses respect as the prerequisite for a rational relationship.

What can one do when faced with powerful authority, or strong, insubordinate rebelliousness?

VERBALIZATION EXAMPLE #5

LESS RATIONAL	MORE RATIONAL

Child (age 8)
(rebelling)
I don't want to finish this work.

Teacher
You had better finish right away or I won't call you to go outside today.

Child
(Sits down reluctantly to work but with hostility and anger.)

Child (age 8)
(rebelling)
I don't want to finish this work.

Teacher
Is this work too hard?

Child
No.

Teacher
Is this work to easy?

Child
Yes.

Teacher
Is this work too boring and long?

Child
Yes.

Teacher
I have observed that on many occasions you spend a lot of time doodling and talking instead of finishing this work. You probably would like to just forget this work and go on to some other thing, don't you?

Child
Yes.

Teacher
Tell me. If you were the teacher, is that what you would do with your students? You would just say to them: "Listen students, if you ever find your work too easy, too

long or too hard, don't bother doing it." Can you imagine what
kind of school that would be?

Child (smiling)
That would not help the students.

Teacher
What do you think is the best way
to deal with long and boring
work? Is it better to goof off and
waste time and keep dragging that
work on and on. day after day?

Child
It's better to get it done and over
with fast.

Teacher
But how can you do that if it's
boring? Do you want to break it
up in parts and say to yourself,
by two o'clock today I'll do this
part; by 10 o'clock tomorrow I can
easily do this much; by the next
day I can finish it all up. Is that
a good plan?

Child
That sounds great. I think I can
manage even more than that.

The technique of verbalizing the child's feelings is of great
importance to establish honest and direct communication. In
being committed to a rational, respectful relationship, one can
never assume anybody's feelings. Yes, the adult must be able
to discover those feelings, be certain of them and verbalize
them correctly so that the child feels visible to the adult rather
than condemned or tolerated with contempt.

The next main problem, after the correct feelings are verbalized is, of course, the problem of what to do with those feelings. It seems fairly easy to be able to understand and verbalize the child's feelings, but knowing what to do afterwards is not always obvious.

As our previous verbalization example points out, empathy (not sympathy) may be the key to respectful relating. Both the teacher and the child become involved in tackling a psychological problem. On one hand, there are the child's negative feelings towards the work; on the other, the intellectual realization that in order to achieve a good skill at anything, practicing is necessary. It's a paradoxical dilemma with which we are all too familiar. Can this dilemma be resolved calmly, without repressing any of the feelings, without either the use of power and authority or by allowing permissiveness and emotionalism?

If both adult and child explore all the avenues and possibilities, they both will discover the best solution to the paradox. Boring and long jobs can be tackled with a different attitude, and the correct attitude can be created. There may be possibilities for accomplishing the task more gradually, at intervals, with the direct help and participation of the teacher. In other words, there is usually a way to turn a lemon into a lemonade.

The joint exploration for a solution for both teacher and child is designed to bring emotions and intellect in alignment with each other, to eliminate the friction between "I want to get away from this boring work," and "I must do it for practice's sake." Intelligence and creativity lie in the ability to bring one's emotions and one's intellect in perfect alignment, without resistance or contradiction.

IV
Developing Self-Motivation

The first aspect of this topic that we need to consider is differentiating between self-motivation, which means motivation from the self or within, and motivation that stems from sources outside ourselves. This is not an easy distinction, as we shall see.

What is the difference between outer and inner motivation? Is it possible to discover for ourselves what self-motivation is? Could we approach it negatively, and through the negative come to a positive definition? Discovery requires that we come to the truth from the negative, obviously, because the process of inquiry begins when one says the negative statement: "I *don't* know." If one were to start with the positive statement "I know," there would be no inquiry at all. It is from the negative that we may come to the positive.

Self-motivation is not the response to a threat, to punishment or a reward, is it? To be valid, self-motivation must be uncontaminated by either punishment or reward.

Is there such a thing? Have we ever come across an action that is not motivated either by fear or by reward? Is there a form of achievement that is not related to reward or punishment?

What is the difference between inner discipline or outer discipline? If at the bottom of it all we always find pleasure or pain, reward or punishment, what is the difference between the inner and outer? Are we just making a big fuss about the difference between inner rewards versus outer rewards, or inner punishment versus outer punishment? Are we not just condoning inner punishments and rewards, but condemning outer punishments and rewards? Obviously pursuing pleasure and avoiding pain is the very essence of the inevitable law of pleasure/pain. It is a movement that accompanies every individual from birth to death.

That direction is set by nature, inescapably. A reward or punishment, whether imposed from others, from society or an authority, or whether it is self-imposed, is still motivation dictated by the pleasure/pain mechanism. After all, what is self-imposed is still the product of conditioning (environment and genetics).

In observing children dispassionately, without prejudice, without the desire to direct our observation to reach preconceived conclusions, we inevitably see the fact that all children perform for rewards and punishments. The rewards or punishments may be self-imposed (and we call these children "self-motivated") or the rewards and punishments may be imposed by others, by some outside authority such as the parents, the teachers, or society.

In either case, rewards and punishments seem to be part of life. Any attempt at doing away with them violates the law of nature itself, it seems. Some children seem to respond better to rewards. Others seem to need more punishment, while others still respond best to a good blend of both.

At this point it seems well worthwhile to come to a good understanding of the terms we are using. Parents and teachers talk and strive in their effort to bring about self-motivation in children. We hear them speak with deep concern of the evils ensuing from a child afflicted by a dreaded syndrome called "unmotivation."

What exactly do we mean by motivation? And is there anything but self-motivation? Isn't any action, any step we take in our life, from the second we wake up in the morning till our last conscious thought before we fall asleep at night, inescapably and choicelessly an act of self-interest? Has anyone seen a child, particularly a child — though an adult is no different — display in any form or degree motivation that does not essentially relate in some way to self-interest? All motivation is necessarily self-motivation, because it is all necessarily dictated by self-interest.

Taken in these terms, trying to develop someone's self-motivation is as contradictory as trying to develop someone's desire in taking the next breath of fresh air. What, then, are parents and teachers all concerned about? They are concerned that what children decide to do may not be in their *best* self-interest in the long run. For example, a child may perceive that playing is in his best self-interest, while learning to spell, to read and write may not have quite the same meaning when compared with having fun. The parent asserts that he is older, more experienced and thus better qualified to decide what is the child's best interest. That's a conflict of interests.

Take spelling. Are there self-motivated children in relation to spelling? Are there children who truly see spelling as being in their best interest? Most children look at spelling as a huge mountain to be climbed. Most children, given the opportunity, would question whether it is actually true that the efforts one must put out to master the subject of English spelling are worth the promised rewards.

Skating, on the other hand, is an activity entirely different from spelling. Children seem to be prepared to put out an enormous spontaneous effort in achieving this skill. In general, they do not perceive skating as a huge mountain to be conquered. We could say that the children are self-motivated to skate, but require much prompting (stimulus, discipline, rewards, punishments) in order to achieve proficiency at spelling. Also, in general, the same expectation is not placed by adults on the achievement of a certain level of skill in skating. Not all children are prepared to apply the kind of effort required in order to become a professional Olympic skater.

If *equal* effort was required by all children in achieving proficiency at skating, many, as it happens with spelling, would opt not to go to the skating rink of their own volition. Like with spelling, many would have to be lured with stimulus and rewards. Others would go only due to fear of punishment.

This is precisely what we do with all children with regard to spelling. We assume that a certain level of ability to spell is required by all children.

What is the intrinsic value of something? Does value lie in punishment or reward? Or is the intrinsic value of something in the rationality of the action itself, its non-contradictory nature. Is there a contradiction in the action of skating? Is there a contradiction in the desire, the pleasure of enjoyment that comes from skating? Of course not. Skating, in most contexts, carries no contradiction for children.

Can spelling be treated in the same way? Have we codified something for others, for the children, that should not be codified and thus get the backlashes from treating something as an obligation instead of a discovery? Could education be devoted not to coercing or bribing children into learning skills, like spelling, but rather to teach the intrinsic value of spelling first? How does one teach such a thing?

Non-contradictory education — rational education — is just beginning to sprout. It is possible to bring children to understand and love school subjects before they can be expected to gain a certain mastery of them. Valuing something, loving a subject comes first. Mastery is a by-product, like success, of an emotional commitment. Only with this attitude can we hope to bring about intelligent individuals in the world. People whose commitment is love for a subject, will inevitably grow to be creative and competent at what they love. Such is the reward of self-motivation.

Were we to really understand the relationship of spelling to the child's life, we would also see that the child understood the value of this skill. Such a motivation then would arise from one's intelligent observation of reality and its action would never be contradictory. Desire would not fight with reason. The child would not have to resist the adult and the short range goal would not contradict the long range goal. This kind of self-motivation is guided by intelligent, rational self-interest. This is the kind of self-motivation worth developing in children.

The key to rational self-motivation lies in educating children to understand the nature of reality and how values are acquired. When we say to the child that spelling is important, whose value are we reciting? Ours, of course. The child is merely being indoctrinated. Rational values, however, are not acquired through indoctrination. Through inculcation we may produce conformity, temporary obedience and, at best, a pleasing, subservient personality.

The long-range results, however, are everything but pleasing. Hypocrisy, dissatisfaction, dullness, fear and hopelessness are but a few of the most obvious consequences derived from a conformity-oriented education.

Understanding that the motivating factor is always a value, we can proceed to distinguish inner values from outer values. Outer values are obviously dictated by outer punishments or rewards, imposed or inculcated by society, parents, teachers, and some other authority.

Just because a value has an inner motive, an inner compulsion, it does not follow that the value is rational. Again, we have come to realize that it is unimportant whether one acts from interior or exterior motives. What really counts is whether or not our motives are objectively valid and therefore free from contradiction.

Rational self-motivation, therefore, is an inner-value that is connected to reality objectively, containing no contradiction. To acquire that understanding is essential in order to prepare the environment, the psychological and physical surroundings necessary to guide the child to living intelligently.

Since all values are products of abstractions, we should examine carefully the abstractions we hold. Abstractions may be valid or invalid, in agreement or in contradiction to reality. To the degree that we are committed to valid abstractions, we hold rational values, which in turn are our best tools for educating children intelligently.

Those of us who work with children know that the children present us with endless opportunities for testing our own rationality. For this reason, the profession of teaching consists much more frequently of exercises in logic and creativity than it consists of academic lessons.

VERBALIZATION EXAMPLE

Ben hates making corrections. I know that corrections are necessary and valuable. Ben doesn't. How do I make such an adult abstraction accessible to the child? The child is a sensorial being. What kind of psychological environment do I prepare for Ben to see the value of making corrections?

Did I first validate the value of corrections within myself completely? What then is the right verbalization that will bring Ben to see the value of making corrections?

LESS RATIONAL

Teacher
These are papers that need to be corrected and returned to me.

Ben (age 7)
I hate to do this. This is too much work.

Teacher
I am sorry but you must always make corrections. Let me explain to you how important corrections are. They help you become very good at your work. How can you really learn without making mistakes and correcting them?

Child
I don't know.

MORE RATIONAL

Teacher
These papers need to be corrected.

Ben (age 7)
I hate corrections.

Teacher
You really hate corrections, don't you?

Ben
Yes.

Teacher
You really would prefer to do new work only, don't you? It would be so nice if we did not have to worry whether the work comes out right or wrong, wouldn't it?

Ben (smiling)
Yes.

Teacher
You would really like to do new work and never have to correct it, don't you?

Ben
Yes.

93

Teacher
If you were the teacher, would you want your students to do that, never to do corrections?

Ben
No.

Teacher
Why? Do you have some good reasons? Why would you ask your students to do corrections?

Ben
Oh . . . well . . . I'd ask the students to do the corrections because they are important. I just don't like to do them myself.

Teacher
I agree with you completely. Which do you think would work better for you: to do a lot of work wrong and then have to correct it? Or to do less work but right from the start?

Ben
I'd rather do less work right the first time.

Teacher
That's what I would choose also. Now, about these corrections, they do need to be made. The best deal I can make you is this: you can do a few corrections today, and a few corrections tomorrow. How many do you feel strong enough to do today?

Ben
Up to here.

Teacher
Good. Are you reserving all the rest for tomorrow?

Ben
Yes.

Teacher
Will you argue with me about this when tomorrow comes?

Ben
No, I won't.

The purpose of this verbalization is to elicit reasoning in the child. This is like having to ask payment from a parent who still owes school tuition two months after the child graduated and left the school. Surprisingly, some adults maintain the same logic that Ben displayed in the example above. They see the necessity of paying the school tuition as long as their child is in school, but if they miss their monthly payments and their child moves on to high school, they do not seem to feel that the remainder of the tuition is validly and objectively owed. Granted, it would be a lot more fun if we could have private schools without having to pay tuition. But, like hoping to learn without having to make any corrections, it stands to reason that one is not possible without the other. Thus, working together on easing their payment schedule becomes an art of creative reasoning very similar to the verbalization example just mentioned.

V
Concentration and Attention:
Two Processes, Two Levels of Awareness

We must distinguish between attention span, which is also understood as concentration, and attention.

The Montessori materials are designed to develop the child's attention span or concentration. In essence, they are a form of stimulus that absorbs the child's energy. The child focuses his attention on the exercise, the concrete apparatus or the task. To the degree that a child stays with his/her task, without being distracted or interrupted by other events and activities in the classroom, we may say that one's attention span is long or short, within the normal range or not.

Dr. Montessori stressed the importance of developing concentration in the child. She stressed the fact that all children must develop this skill and that her materials were conceived with this purpose in mind. The child has a need to become absorbed by the materials and concentrate.

A small baby, by nature, is easily distracted. Eye-hand coordination is a skill that must be achieved after a period of practice, and by trial and error. Becoming absorbed by a toy, or by the mother's smiling face, or by a dog's wagging tail, or by the hustle and bustle of a busy market place, are but a few of the thousands of ways in which a child learns to coordinate all his senses in concert with his developing mind. His vision responds to his auditory and tactile senses, then with the olfactory and gustatory senses.

This ability to focus one's attention as a response to sensory stimulus, however, is only the necessary beginning for developing broader attention or awareness.

One of the abnormal consequences of hyperactivity is indeed the inability of an older child to remain with one's activity for a reasonable length of time. Instead, such a child tends to move from unfinished task to unfinished task, from one stimulus to another, restlessly seeking ever growing stimuli in number and intensity. The ability to concentrate, for such a child, is strictly dependent on the newness or intensity of the stimulus.

Typically, the Montessori environment is designed to correct this problem, not by appealing to higher and higher forms of stimulus but, on the contrary, by reducing the quantity of sensory and mental input and offering children a quiet, soothing place where they must combine intellectually self-motivated purposes with sensory-oriented apparatus and activities. All types of children benefit from such scientific preparation of the environment, not just the hyperactive ones.

It is important to understand the biological implication of words such as "focusing," "concentration," or "attention." At the most obvious superficial level we can observe that one focuses or concentrates when some form of stimulus operates to attract one's awareness in a specific direction. The newness and intensity of the event or stimulus is often the only cause of such directed attention.

At a deeper level, one's intellectual evaluation of the events or stimuli provides the self-motivating impetus for attention to take place. Attention is a deeper process than concentration precisely because the intellectual evaluation of whatever attracts us plays an even greater part than the sensory response.

While concentration is primarily dependent on the outside stimulus and is necessarily exclusive to be effective, attention is the product of conscious evaluation, and provides a broader level of awareness. A child needs to develop both concentration and attention.

In attention, focusing and concentrating are included. In concentration, attention is not included. In attention one is aware that focusing and concentrating impose limits on our scope of awareness. The process of attention, on the other hand, is limitless and should be emphasized over the process of concentration. Attention allows the discovery of indefinite implications and connections. Concentration is most efficient if it is narrow and fixed.

Understanding the difference between these processes helps us develop two different forms of verbalizations and two different ways of interacting with children.

We must know what to say to children depending on whether we are trying to develop concentration or attention. A child who can easily concentrate has not completed the task of awareness. Most children who can concentrate well at a young age are unwittingly deceptive to both teachers and parents. They present no visible problem for the adults, but they frequently lack the ability to know themselves and, most importantly, lack the opportunity to learn about themselves in relationship.

Typically, children who cannot concentrate are emotionally immature and present a variety of obvious problems and challenges in relationship with adults and peers. They cannot be ignored. These children never lack opportunities for interaction. They learn, for better or for worse, how to relate with people of all kinds. If we are to give all children the best opportunity for developing the skills necessary for relating rationally, our understanding of these concepts becomes essential.

To develop the child's concentration-span is as necessary a skill as learning to speak, but learning to speak is not the end of education: it is merely the beginning. Similarly, learning to concentrate is a prerequisite skill to become educated, but it is not education. Education deepens with attention.

With attention, the child's intellect participates in the understanding of the many implications arising by interacting both with people and the environment.

What, exactly, is distraction? We often call the child's act of being totally absorbed in building the pink tower an act of *concentration*. By the same standard, we call the child's act of watching people and cars come and go in the parking lot, for example, an act of *distraction*. But the two processes are intrinsically identical. Their difference lies not in the process but in the objects.

Such distinction between what constitutes an act of concentration and an act of distraction is invalid, of course, because it is purely arbitrary. The adult determines that attention directed to the pink tower exercise is to be considered concentration, while attention directed to the traffic in the school parking lot is to be considered distraction.

From the teacher's viewpoint, one is a desirable activity (building the pink tower), while the other is not desirable (wasting time watching the traffic in the parking lot). Both are sensory stimuli. Both originate from the environment and both may have a various degree of intensity and attractiveness.

In teaching children to acquire the skill of concentration we dare not violate the rules of logic. Concentration is useful and valuable in order to achieve a specific goal. For example, if one must do some calculations, one must have a reasonable quiet environment for such an activity. The exclusion of certain noises, music or human voices may be important for the successful completion of certain hard intellectual tasks. The contradictory aspect comes into play when one cannot have such exclusive environment, but one still attempts the tasks.

There is a strong sense of resistance and a tendency to resent the noises, the voices, the distractions. Similarly, in the education of children, we must understand that they are more susceptible to stimuli than we are. To demand concentration in a highly stimulating environment is irritating for both the child and the adult.

Attention, however, is never contradictory or divisive. As a teacher, one must learn to provide support for the child, not only in achieving concentration, but in being attentive to the so called distractions, so that the child may independently learn to interact with the environment according to rational values, not arbitrary ones.

It is necessary to differentiate the type of verbalization that helps a child learn about attention from the type of verbalization that merely brings about concentration by means of stimulus or fear and, therefore, through contradiction.

Most of us have been taught that you cannot be attentive without repressing "distractions," which means that paying attention is understood only as concentration on one particular task at the exclusion of other input. Although this is desirable at times in order to be efficient at completing a task, it is not the normal state of awareness one needs to have in order to be efficient (intelligent) at living in general. Open channels of reception to the whole of possible sensory perception are desirable for creativity, broader awareness and ultimately efficient, non-contradictory living.

VERBALIZATION EXAMPLE #1

Mark (age 3) brings an old key from home each day he comes to school. He will not part from the key at the door. His parents will ask him to give it to them for safe keeping, but he wants to keep it in his pocket. From time to time, unexpectedly, Mark takes the key out of his pocket during class. Sometimes he misplaces it. The teacher has pointed out that the key is an unnecessary source of disturbance.

LESS RATIONAL

Teacher
Mark, you must leave the key with me.

Mark
No, no! I want my key.

Teacher
You can have the key, but I expect you to keep it in your pocket and not take it out.

Mark
OK.

(The child cannot resist taking it out of his pocket later in the day. The teacher must carry out a disciplinary action without the child's full understanding.)

MORE RATIONAL

Teacher
I see that Mark has his key with him today. What are you going to do with it, Mark?

Mark
I don't know.

Teacher
This is the time and place where your key must not be seen. Can you keep it in your pocket or do you prefer that I keep it for you?

Mark
I'll keep it in my pocket.

Teacher
It is very difficult to keep your key in the pocket and out of sight for the whole day. What will happen if Mark takes out the key during class? Can we agree that if I see the key you will give it to me to keep for the rest of the day?

Mark
Yes.

As the teacher learns about the difference between concentration and attention, one begins to understand that attention yields far more benefits than concentration. As one becomes attentive to the needs and interests of the children, the children learn to be attentive to the needs and interests of the adults. This kind of attention, which is really awareness in relationship, provides the condition for mutual respect.

Spontaneously, as the adult applies scientific, objective observation to the needs and interests of the children, the children learn to apply such an observation, too. In this way, indirectly, without a formal lesson, we can transfer to the child the quality of being a scientific observer, an objective observer, and therefore an individual with awareness and sensitivity for the environment and those in it.

By developing attention, understood here as broad awareness and sensitivity for the condition in which we live (the classroom environment), we can develop, as a natural consequence, the correct verbalizations, the correct techniques which are suitable and appropriate for a rational form of relationship.

We know that focusing is frequently a response to adult's reprimanding: "Don't look over there. Look at this project. Pay attention to this lesson." Concentration generally implies exclusion and the verbalizations used to bring it about and sustain it are usually authoritarian, divisive and contradictory.

Attention, on the other hand, yields non-contradictory statements, sensitive, thoughtful verbalizations that leave room for a dialogue, an interaction. There is a gentleness and thoughtfulness peculiar to attention. In attention there is not power and authority, but a natural sense of curiosity through inquiry and questioning, so distinctive of human intelligence.

A statement such as: "I am watching how you carry the tray" does not imply authority, fear or contradictory denial over other stimuli. The awareness of how a child carries a tray joins the awareness of how the teacher is watching. A statement such as: "Don't look over there, watch your tray!" implies concentration at the expense of attention.

There are many possibilities in attention. The verbalizations vary like the patterns of a kaleidoscope. Each may be just slightly different from the others, and one small difference may be the cause of subtle and meaningful implications.

To develop attention (awareness), a teacher must strive to achieve the wider, broader possible degree of implications. It is within this broad attention that the best possible verbalizations of respect and rational relationship may spontaneously arise.

VERBALIZATION EXAMPLE #2

Here is a child (age 3) carrying a tray and in the process of carrying he gets distracted. Instead of maintaining attention to the direction he is walking, he is turning his face to another direction . . . but he keeps on walking. He is likely to crash or trip and the teacher is aware of the whole event as it is taking place.

What is the rational response of the teacher to this situation?

a) Verbally or by gentle touch the teacher warns the child of the imminent possible crash: "Jerry, watch where you are going! You were just about ready to crash into this child."

(The teacher's awareness is immediately transferred to the child.)

b) Verbalize options of behavior one could choose from: "When you carry something and something else attracts your attention away from your carrying, what can you do? Which of these choices is better for you?

1. Walk on with your head turned away.

2. Stop walking and freely look at what attracts your attention, then resume walking by watching where you are going."

The most appropriate answer is the one that adheres to the specific context we are experiencing and produces no contradiction. By providing children with this approach, we are paving the way to developing their objective observation and their total awareness of the appropriateness of their behavior in each moment. That process of broad awareness of what is appropriate for each moment is what I call *attention.*

While children of preschool age must be taught to develop attention on an uninterrupted manner, from the moment they wake up in the morning to the moment they go to sleep at night, the older children, approximately from age six and up, may have learned self-destructive patterns of thinking that sabotage their ability to be fully aware of this difference between younger children and older ones. That awareness, too, will cause appropriate verbalizations to ensue for each specific event.

If an older child knows that attention is necessary, but has learned to ignore or avoid thinking about the consequences of certain behaviors or events, the adult must be prompt to intervene. The teacher must point out the various options open to the child and the advantages and disadvantages associated with each option until the child may independently abstract why one option is indeed preferable and non-contradictory. That option will be where attention, sensitivity, logic and rationality are.

What does it mean to prepare students for the "real" world? We often hear parents say that the Montessori approach is wonderful and helpful to protect the child from negative influences or irrationality in general. But the parents know all too well that sooner or later their child will have to meet that world out there — the world of authoritarianism, the world of bullies, the world of power and competition. They refer to that world as the "real world" as though protecting their child was part of fantasy, a temporary fairyland. Can one really prepare children for that "real world?"

I say that the question is invalid and therefore no answer can be adequate. One does not and cannot "protect" a child and then, at a certain age, throw that child to the wolves. Protection has meaning only if in the process of protecting one knows how to teach that child how to enter the world of corruption, injustice, deception, power and abuse without becoming part of it, without being touched by the irrational madness that is around us. Then, and only then, will education have been meaningful. Only with this goal in mind one can prepare children to live in this world.

Surely no responsible adult recommends early exposure to deception and corruption in order to prepare children for life. And surely complete removal from daily life is not the answer to preparing to cope with the challenges of the modern world. The challenge of education is to prepare people to meet the irrational from day one.

From the moment the child begins to ask the first questions about life, the challenge of the educator is to help him understand how to cope with the irrational. How, then, can one prepare the child to observe that which is contradictory without the risk that the child might accept it, justify it and become part of it?

We do not need to prepare children to meet that which is rational. That presents no challenge at all. Educators must be committed to prepare children to meet the irrational. If a child in a Montessori environment is shown how to observe life in general (human interaction in particular) in an objective manner, then that child will grow with sensitivity and awareness, will develop attention and know what it means to be attentive.

By the time that child reaches the high school age, he will move into the traditional approach, a ruthless system (as it currently is) of classifying people according to conformism, not individuality. This is notoriously a highly irrational system, governed by arbitrary and illogical ways of dealing with the process of developing human minds.

How will our Montessori students respond to that world? Will the years spent in learning to relate rationally, with attention, go completely to waste? I support the view that we must learn to live in a world surrounded by the irrational and that it will be our ability to be attentive and aware of all the dangers that will help us meet the challenges intelligently and avoid all psychological traps. Without that supreme capability (which can only come from rational education) the young individual will be lost and to one degree or another, will be inevitably absorbed by the quagmire of irrationality.

Before a child can be equipped to cross the tremendous jungle of the irrational, he must receive plenty of attention, plenty of time to acquire the knowledge and the necessary skills for this very dangerous journey. A rational Montessori school environment, not only protects the young child from premature exposure to irrationality, but it supplies the very tools needed to counteract the effects of the irrational when the individual will have no alternative environments to live in. Therefore, my strongest recommendation to all parents is that their children enter the traditional approach of education as late as possible in life.

VI
Fostering Self-Esteem

Self-esteem is defined as the *objective* evaluation we have of ourselves with regard to competence at living. More concretely, our self-esteem measures how rational we consider ourselves to be. Pseudo-self-esteem, on the other hand, is the act of evaluating ourselves basing our judgment on what pleases us or on how we wish to appear.

As teachers, we must realize that nothing can be passed to the children that we ourselves do not first possess. Self-esteem is no exception to this rule. Before we can hope to provide guidance to the children in acquiring their self-esteem, it will be necessary that we find out exactly what level of self-esteem we ourselves have acquired.

By understanding that psychological security cannot be forced either upon oneself or upon others, one becomes aware that self-esteem is the logical consequence of a profound commitment to one's own rational thinking. For this purpose, an effective tool for looking into our thoughts is the negative process. Amazingly, if we start examining our thoughts from a negative approach, we shall discover, by contrast, what the positive actually is.

A negative approach begins when we become conscious of certain facts:

a) we lack adequate self-esteem
b) we are generally psychologically insecure
c) we are generally psychologically dependent

We can become free from our limitations only when they are fully understood. Wishing to become psychologically secure and independent is not sufficient, in itself, to bring about such qualities. By studying the feelings of insecurity and dependence within ourselves we are faced with studying a very complex algebraic equation about the psychology of the human being in general. And in studying what dependence is and all its implications one discovers what independence is. Similarly, by studying psychological insecurity, we naturally discover and acquire psychological security and self-esteem.

Obviously, dependence and insecurity have a lot to do with the way one was brought up as a child. Those feelings become part of the pattern one uses in dealing with life. They become part of the personality. Our personality is the product of the genes as well as the product of the environment in which we were educated. Some dependence has genetic roots. Some of it was produced by the environment in the way we were educated.

Where should our study start? Our study should start with the most obvious and easiest area: the behavioral patterns we acquired from the way we were brought up.

When we realize that most of our attitudes are the result of the way our parents brought us up, what can we do about it? Most of us react against our past, instead of studying it. We may promise ourselves never to raise our children in the way we were brought up, or, we may accept our parents' model. Either decision will not help us understand our past and how psychological dependence is perpetuated.

Only a dispassionate study of psychological dependence can reveal to us the irrational foundation on which our behavioral patterns are based. Dr. Montessori used to call any such abnormality of behavior a *deviation*, a very appropriate term for it. In every manifestation of psychological dependence there is a message: an impulse to either rebel against what one was taught, or accept it and conform in order to feel secure. Therefore, through psychological dependence we can never teach the value of objective inquiry.

We cannot even discover whether our actions are rational or irrational. Psychological dependence can actually prevent us from finding out the truth about ourselves because it always supports authority and power, either through rejection (violence) or through acceptance (conformism).

Studying one's psychological dependence involves observing oneself in relationship to others. Such a study will reveal the values we have learned to *accept* and the values we have learned to *reject*. It will also point out the new values, those we created for ourselves. This observation implies an objective and dispassionate study of how one reasons.

The reward of this kind of observation is self-knowledge. Self-knowledge cannot be learned through books or be passed on to us by someone else. In learning how to be independent and how to think rationally lies the key to freedom from previous conditioning.

The emotional child within us has not fully grown to maturity. That child in us is the root of our psychological dependence. In studying all of its facets, there arises freedom. Thus, understanding dependence is the essence of independence and the beginning of self-esteem.

Most frequently, we experience self-esteem as competence related to the activities that we consciously choose because we can perform them well. It is for this reason that self-confidence on the job does not always translate into self-confidence in other areas of one's life, such as traveling, meeting new people, learning new subjects, public speaking, etc. We are referring in this case to a compartmentalized form of self-esteem. But the type of self-esteem we are advocating here is not a compartmentalized competence in some skill. Here, by the word "self-esteem" we want to indicate the sum total of a person's acquired ability to live rationally, that is, our competence at living.

Lack of self-esteem expressed as psychological dependence may occur only in relationship, not in the technical knowledge or in the fields of specializations. Let's observe psychological dependence at work within the mind of a small child, for example. Imagine that you had to explain to a happy child that his parents have died suddenly in an accident. Such an unfortunate child would probably have thoughts similar to these:

"I miss my parents. My life is coming to an end. I can never be happy again."

"I don't know who will take care of me, now. Perhaps some mean people will look after me. No one can love me like my parents did. I feel so lonely and helpless."

Those are the thoughts of fear in a child. They are certainly appropriate for a child in this predicament. These thoughts, however, are not appropriate during life's normal conditions. Yet, many people hold similiar thoughts as adults when confronted with having to make decisions during circumstances not nearly as traumatic as the loss of a loved one. People often grow up fearing change, whether it is moving to a new part of the country, or changing a job. The purpose of education is to prepare the child to be both physically and emotionally independent.

It is possible to create an environment, both physical and psychological, that is scientifically conducive to maturity and independence. Without this kind of commitment, education has little meaning. The traditional approach has failed to give children this important aspect of their emotional development and the devastating consequences of neurosis, insecurity and general lack of competence at living rationally are visible all around us.

It is a biological fact that the child wants to pursue pleasure and to escape pain. Though this biological law has served the animals well (it tells animals instinctively how to satisfy their physical needs in a naturally ordained environment in which the survival of the fittest is almost always assured), this same rule is only partially effective with humans, particularly with physically and psychologically dependent children. Without the care of the parents or some surrogate parent, the small child, even when capable of feeding himself, would very likely perish, unable to meet his most fundamental physical needs.

Should an orphan child be lucky to survive in the wilderness by scavenging and foraging as some primitive people did, his mental capacity (as shown by Jean Itard's accounts)* would very much resemble that of an animal, rather than that of a human being. Thus, the ability of such a child to interact with other members of the species in our modern, complex society would be severely handicapped.

---

* Jean Itard, *L'Enfant Sauvage d'Aveyron* (Wild Boy of Aveyron). New York, Appleton-Century-Crofts, 1962.

For these most basic reasons, educating children about human (rational) living is most essential. But education has meaning *only* if the adult has understood and is capable to explain to the child how the law of pleasure/pain works in harmony with rationality as the basic standard of all life. We could summarize the greatest lesson an adult could pass on to a child as this: **To pursue pleasure and avoid pain is perfectly right and natural as long as such pursuit does not yield contradiction.**

Indeed, simple as this lesson may seem, it is hardly mastered by young and old alike. In countless ways, events and daily activities challenge the human mind for the application of this principle, a principle on which non-contradictory decisions and rational living rest.

Is there a school for children, or a university for adults, where one can study and learn to apply the principles of non-contradictory living? Education is fundamentally worthless without considering this primary aspect. Children are taught how to read, write and compute. Yet, information and misinformation are widely disseminated with equal zeal by schools and the media, often making it hard for the recipients to distinguish one from the other.

There is a great need to create places where learning to live rationally is the main subject and where all other subjects are secondary and consistent with the essential goal of education. If education cannot produce individuals with integrity, sane and rational, whether they know how to read and compute or not has very little meaning.

At variance with religious and mystical studies, which tend to be either extremely recondite or function as a collection of popularized fairy tales, the study of rational living requires no leap of blind faith, no allegiance to any group or organization. The individual is asked to be in direct contact with reality and he reigns as the ultimate authority. His mind bows to no one on account of any prejudice, be it race, nationality, religious belief, sex or socio-economic level.

It is this kind of understanding that constitutes the spiritual preparation of a true leader, and the Montessori approach is the perfect vehicle where intelligence and rational living may be practiced by both teachers and students.

The traditional system of education, with its emphasis on standardized grades and classifying students based on conformity and group average, has for centuries denied the individual the status of sovereignty to which each person is naturally entitled. As the young child, from kindergarten through grade school, is taught to belong and conform to the group, he is also taught that power and authority are to be bowed to, regardless of rationality.

This approach, so well rooted in all traditional, group-oriented classes is inconsistent with the Montessori method and it is perhaps the most fundamental difference that inspired E. M. Standing, a close collaborator of Dr. Montessori, to identify the Montessori method as a "quiet revolution" now under way in mankind's history of education. It naturally follows that it will be up to single individuals — not organizations — to carry out the quiet revolution that both Dr. Montessori and E. M. Standing envisioned. Unfortunately, though the seeds are all there, few individuals, even within the Montessori movement, seem currently capable of bringing this crucial point to maturity and to the forefront of the field of education.

QUESTION AND ANSWER DIALOGUE

Student Teacher:
Sometimes children refuse to cooperate. They'll flatly rebel against the authority. What can one do to bring about good communication and meet this challenge?

Mr A:
A child who says: "No, I won't do this," is a child who is rebelling against authority. At that point, we have reached a confrontation. No matter which direction we take, we have already lost communication.

If I say: "You will do this work, because I will see that you be punished, or some privileges be taken away from you if you don't," my actions are part of the confrontation. I am displaying my power and going to war. I probably will get what *I want*, but I will not have achieved communication.

If I say: "Oh well, if you feel that strongly about it, put it away and do it another time," I am being permissive and I'll be sending a message to the child that indicates that he is getting his way when he uses power. The child gets what *he wants*, but I still have not achieved communication. Is there a right course of action that one can take in this circumstance?

In confrontation, the general principle to remember is to de-escalate, to find ways to reduce the tension and bring people to the same emotional level. Verbalizing feelings always de-escalates.

A temper-tantrum is a mini-rebellion. It always stems from repression or license. By the time people reach the level of a confrontation, the point of communication has passed. At that point, re-establishing communication is the main goal of rationality.

What are the dominant emotions that need to be verbalized during a confrontation? They are usually emotions of frustration, hostility, anger and even hatred.

This is what happens at the level of political revolutions with countries. At the individual level, a teacher still has the opportunity to use rationality to de-escalate a confrontation.

112

VERBALIZATION EXAMPLE

LESS RATIONAL	MORE RATIONAL

LESS RATIONAL

Student (age 6-11)
I am not going to read.

Teacher
Oh yes you will!

Student
No, I won't! I won't!

Teacher
You can either do the reading now, or you'll have to sit aside and I won't call you back until you decide to do your reading exercise. Also, I am not going to allow you to do your art project until you do this work.

Student
I don't care.

MORE RATIONAL

Student (age 6-11)
I am not going to read.

Teacher
You really hate reading with me, don't you?

Student
I just don't like reading these stories. They are too hard for me.

Teacher
These are very hard stories. They are not for small children, you are right. How about if I read the first sentence for you first, so that you can tell which are the hardest words before reading it back to me?

Student
OK.

VII
Eliminating Peer Rivalry
and
Unhealthy Competition

To compete means to strive for a prize or for profit against someone else. In a game, competition implies winning over an opponent. Many people, observing the brutality of competition in the adult world of business and politics, teach their children to shun from it. They choose safe niches in life, both for themselves and for their children, where rewards are small and simple and the risks are minimal.

But competition is all around us in the world, both in nature and in our so-called civilized society. What does competition imply?

We learn that one can be more skillful than another. A child can run faster, learn faster, have better qualities than another. Regardless of how hard one child tries to improve a certain skill, there is always the possibility that someone can be faster, greater and better. Is it correct, therefore, to teach children to compete with one another so that becoming better is a new value to be pursued?

Why is it so important that one be better than others? We can understand wanting to improve our own skills, pursuing excellence as a goal in itself. The traditional system has consistently used competition among peers as a pedagogical technique to achieve competence. But can competence be achieved through competing?

Having to compete with another pushes us to practice in order to win. By practicing, we inevitably become more skillful. So, we ought to conclude that competition, used as a technique, does work in many cases in producing a desired level of skill and competence.

We see this technique well at work particularly in competitive sports. But could a skill be achieved independently from competition?

There is a contradiction in the concept of competition. Two values vie with each other. One is the healthy value of improving one's skill; the other is the psychological pleasure we derive when we win over others, that is, the feeling of admiration and importance.

It is difficult to distinguish clearly which is the predominant motive in a competitive person. Are we competing to improve our skill, or are we competing to achieve fame, prestige, status. In the latter case, the acquisition of competence is not an end in itself. A skill becomes the means to the fulfillment of a psychological need, and as such it is contradictory and unhealthy. That psychological need indicates the profound spiritual emptiness within. In an effort to fill that emptiness, we actually use competition to cover up and deny the reality of our psychological inadequacy.

Is there a healthy form of competition? Surely competitive sports do not necessarily imply psychological inadequacy. If you practice a sport as a game or as a form of recreation, competition is itself part of the game. Thus, as long as competition is never linked to self-esteem, there is a place for healthy competition. When competition is completely removed from self-esteem, we can enjoy it without being psychologically dependent on winning or losing. With this attitude, the word sportsmanship has meaning.

One of the ways a teacher may evaluate the psychological health of a student is precisely to observe a student's sense of sportsmanship. Can the student lose a sport event graciously and be capable of objective self-evaluation? Can such a student happily recognize the superiority of the opponent without malice, but with respect and admiration? If he can compete without letting winning or losing go to his head, without self-engrandizement or self-belittlement, then such is the degree of sportsmanship — the degree of objectivity.

QUESTION AND ANSWER DIALOGUE

Student Teacher:

I have a question about peer rivalry and competition in the way I experience this problem with the children in my class. I would like to know what my response ought to be when I find the children bragging to one another about their reading assignments or their levels. They'd say something like this to one another: "I am past you in this; I am ahead of you in this lab."

Mr. A:

This is a typical situation where peer rivalry and competition are at work to fulfill a psychological need that most children have. Early in their development, children derive pleasure from recognition and acceptance by the adults around them. This pattern is usually consciously or unconsciously reinforced, and the children grow up with a need for recognition that seems natural and an inseparable part of their being. Reinforced in a thousand subtle ways, eventually children seek recognition even if it means putting someone else down and showing off their accomplishments.

One must recognize that no matter how common, how widespread this pattern of behavior is, it is still a deviation. What can a teacher do to expose this deviation exactly for what it is to the child himself? We must observe this behavior in all its aspects and consequences.

Does it bring about friendship, closeness, cooperation, enjoyment among the children? Obviously not.

If its consequences are antagonism, intimidation, conflict, suspicion, insecurity and fear, how do we expose all this to the children so that they understand what they are doing to one another and voluntarily stop? Can they be taught to understand rivalry and end it without a reward or a punishment?

The teacher's verbalization must be well thought out in order to be rational or effective. They must address the emotions the children feel for one another without the slightest distortion, without praise or reproach for one child or the other.

116

The teacher's verbalizations should be objective, unemotional, descriptive of the reality of the feelings of the children. The teacher would not, for example, preach and moralize to the children, expounding on the merits of sensitivity to one another, or reciting commandments and rules the children should learn and follow.

Before we can tell the children anything about their feelings, we must delve into our own minds and look at competition with all its ramifications dispassionately. What is competition? What is rivalry at the emotional level? What do these things mean or have meant to me? If I can find out what my feelings are in relation to these situations, then I instantaneously would know what to say to the children, because my feelings and theirs are not different.

Rivalry and competition stem from a tremendous desire for recognition, for attention, often for affection. If a child always seems to point out how much more ahead he or she is over someone else, how much better, how much longer, or greater his or her work is than someone else's, what does that mean emotionally? The child wants love, recognition and attention. The child is saying: "Look how good I am, notice me, admire me, love me." Ultimately, the need is for affection. The child has made the association that being the best means being loved the most.

Desire, like thirst, can only diminish if it is fully quenched. A child's need for affection and recognition can be met if the child deals with it intelligently, rationally, objectively. One must be dispassionate, unemotional to meet this challenge correctly. One must study, observe and think the problem through as though one was trying to solve the most complex algebraic equation. With that approach, not eager to give a quick answer, without offering a hasty bromide to simply repress the child's emotion, it is possible to quench the child's desire for affection without reinforcing rivalry and competition, and without driving his feelings underground.

VERBALIZATION EXAMPLE

LESS RATIONAL

Chris (age 9)
I am ahead of Elizabeth.

Teacher
It's not important to be ahead of someone else. It is important that you do your best work. We don't want to hurt Elizabeth's feelings.

Elizabeth
But I'll be ahead of you tomorrow, when I'll do my assignment.

MORE RATIONAL

Chris (age 9)
I am ahead of Elizabeth.

Teacher
Does being ahead of Elizabeth make you feel more important in the class?

Chris
Well . . . no.

Teacher
But it's a good feeling to be ahead of her, isn't it?

Chris
Yes.

Teacher
Does someone think more of you if you are ahead of Elizabeth?

Chris
No.

Teacher
You know, Chris, I like you and think you are a fine boy whether you are ahead or behind her. Did you know that?

Chris
Yes.

VIII
Violence/Aggressiveness: Aspects of Insecurity

Violence begins with disrespect. When one experiences force, compulsion or obligation one resists. That resistance is conflict. Disrespect is resistance directed towards something or somebody. The child who perceives that the adult is using force in some form or another inevitably begins to resist. That resistance may start with an argument, it may continue as verbal abuse, aggressive or rebellious behavior until it may reach physical violence.

To eliminate violence, one must understand completely the issue of respect. Respect means order in relationship. It means that two people understand fundamentally their identity. Human beings are essentially identical in their needs and it is precisely because people's fundamental needs are identical that communication is possible.

On the basis of this identity, people can respect one another. Respect deepens when one admires the rational behavior or achievements of another.

It's possible to educate children to understand the fundamental importance of respect both as communication and as admiration of rational goals and achievements. Without understanding respect, abuse and violence cannot be removed.

The compulsion to use force may arise from feelings of self-importance (the conviction that one has a righteous mission to accomplish), or from feelings of frustration and anger (reacting against something or somebody standing as an obstacle in our way). In educating children to see themselves as intelligent, rational human beings, one must study the process of violence, observe its roots of origin and think all the possibilities through.

In feeling angry, we have the desire to act out our anger in a destructive way. And it would be only by acting out our anger that violence would take place.

Acknowledging our anger or frustration is not violence. Emotions, such as frustration or anger, arise independently of our will. We are powerless with regard to their presence. Neither denial nor control will eliminate our emotions. Emotions are felt, but not chosen. If we observe the amazing process of emotions very carefully, we will find out that they, not we, seem to have a will of their own, as though they were choosing us, and not the reverse. Indeed, they may possess us, but they have no ability to understand us; we, on the other hand, can understand them. Observing and studying these emotions is essential to understanding them and through understanding we can establish order and rationality.

The following steps may provide a helpful guideline in the understanding of aggressiveness as it arises:

a) Acknowledging feelings
b) Observing and studying feelings
c) Fantasizing solutions through violence
d) Observing feelings dwindle and disappear.

These are steps we must practice within ourselves before we can attempt to have children follow them. We can then feel angry, but we do not have to act on that feeling. Observing and studying our anger is the only way to reach alternative rational solutions to the problems of violence.

QUESTION AND ANSWER DIALOGUE

Student Teacher:

In our school we have a student, a three-year old girl, who is aggressive both with adults and with children. Anne screams and yells and throws incredible temper-tantrums when she doesn't get her way. Often, even when she does. Most adults have learned to back off and let her throw a fit until she exhausts herself and becomes more sensible. She is often tired and antagonistic at the time she arrives at school.

She perceives adults as being automatically against her. She copes with authority by defying it. She thinks all adults are against her and she is permanently on guard. The only expression appropriate for her fear of authority is anger and throwing fits. She is contrary, recalcitrant and often fights no matter what one says. She is constantly prepared for war.

Mr. A:

With a child like this, one ought to know more about the home background and how a pattern like this has developed at such a young age. However, our general principles ought to work regardless what the concrete situation at home is.

The first thing we should establish is our goal. What specifically do we want to accomplish? Let's describe it to ourselves. We probably would like to see Anne change from this aggressive, fearful little girl into a calm, quiet, reasonable child.

The next question is not how we are going to do that. But why would Anne want to be a new kind of child instead of the old angry one? What does she have to gain in becoming this polite, respectful little girl?

If a child perceives adults as attackers, it is logical to expect a permanent defense system. Anne has obviously learned at a young age that her dignity and integrity can only be preserved by fighting and defending.

Student Teacher:

In fact, when she screams, her whole expression seems to convey this message: "Respect me. Stop abusing me!"

Mr. A:

Since all human action and behavior is the product of abstraction, we must dwell on this principle and surmise that Anne's behavior is no exception. The next principle we must bear in mind is that all abstractions depend on the pleasure/pain mechanism. We do not reach a certain abstraction independent from life's all encompassing law of pleasure/pain mechanism. We strive to abstract because we are convinced that the pursuit of the intellect is going to reveal more knowledge, more autonomy, more opportunity to either improve our life condition or achieve non-contradictory pleasure. So, we want to abstract in order to achieve more pleasure, hopefully, more rational and more non-contradictory pleasure.

Can Anne understand that not all adults are interested in pushing her around and that it is not necessary to fight and scream to preserve one's dignity? How is she going to see this truth, this new abstraction? And has this been a real, consistent truth for her in her actual interaction with adults? Obviously not.

Let's begin with respect. This is a child who needs to experience concretely a sense of trust, a sense of consistent protection from at least one adult in her life. She needs an enormous amount of respect. Respect carries its own reward. Anne needs to see that respect is related to pleasure, rational pleasure, of course. She needs to come to the abstraction that adults can relate with her without posing a threat to her dignity.

How can she come to this new abstraction? Why would she want to achieve this new way of relating? Naturally, all her abstractions stem from past experiences. We can safely assume that being at peace with herself and calmly listening to adults' instructions are not behaviors she learned to value. Yet, this is what she must do as a first step: she must come to value a new form of behavior and a new sense of relating with people. She will only come to it if the adult is capable of showing her affection and protection, perhaps as an exchange. The adult must first study this child's reasoning.

What does Anne value? Can we make a list of what we know are her values?

Student Teacher:

As a teacher, I am familiar with what Anne values. She likes:

— coloring
— cutting and pasting
— feeding the fish
— feeding the hamster
— taking messages from teacher to office
— going outside to play

Mr. A:

No technique can work on a long range basis without someone taking full responsibility to be committed to applying rational principles.

Most likely, in the home environment, this child is being treated rather impersonally, probably without much dignity. Most of the time, at school, she must share time and affection with many other children. Her behavior, on the other hand, indicates a great need for closeness to one person and for affection. Therefore, there must be one adult who takes Anne as his or her consistent responsibility in trying to develop a trustworthy relationship. Such a person will be successful if he or she dedicates a personal commitment to applying the proper techniques (exchanging values and dramatization) on a consistent basis.

Aggressive behavior is often the result of frustration. In the classroom one may encounter the fact that younger children can present a problem for older ones. They may interfere with the values of older, but immature, students who are impatient with the behavior of younger students. This is not different from the experience that many siblings encounter at home, where the disparity of values, due to different interests and ages, can cause antagonism.

The interests and values of the older children are frequently unwittingly trampled over by the interests and behaviors of younger children. In most cases, this occurs because the younger child is naturally curious about the activities of the older ones.

The desire to imitate is so strong that it often leads the young child to become involved in projects, activities or behaviors outside the normal scope of one's age. This infringement of unspoken rules of age boundaries is often the cause for disciplinary action on the part of older children and siblings.

The reverse can also happen when an older child demonstrates lack of sensitivity by disregarding the values and activities of his younger peers.

Adults often think that age segregation is the best answer in the solution of this problem. In fact, many adults believe that the root of the problem of aggressiveness and antagonism is the intolerance that children of different ages frequently display for one another. By providing social situations applicable to a particular age group and by grouping school children in classrooms where age limits are strictly compressed into grade levels, it was hoped that, among other benefits, aggressiveness and antagonism would naturally vanish.

Children of the same age, perhaps for very different reasons, display aggressiveness, intolerance and mutual disrespect just as much as children of varying ages. The key to eliminating behavioral antagonism is more likely to be found in the construction of human intelligence than in the matter of age similarity or disparity.

Dr. Montessori looked at the child from birth on as the "constructor of man" within himself. She looked at the destiny of the child in his highest possible form: a sane, mature, rational human being. Maturity and rationality were to be considered the normal attributes of an adult individual. It followed that everything short of this goal should be understood as either a limitation to the construction of the self or a deviation from normality.

If we, like Dr. Montessori, begin with normality as the standard (normality here is intended as the most mature, the most rational), then we can begin to understand the broad meaning that Montessori ascribed to the word "deviation."

Without beginning with a firm concept of normality, it is not possible to be scientific in our observation of human behavior. It is for this reason that most of us, not knowing how to distinguish the normal from the abnormal, have learned to accept irrational behavior as normal, simply because it is so commonly displayed. Throwing temper-tantrums, being abusive, being shy and excessively withdrawn, no matter how frequently a child displays these forms of behavior, can never become normal forms of behavior.

It is a mistake of the adult to adjust and accept children with their limitations and deviations as though they were intrinsic aspects of the individual. Limitations and deviations should not be considered temporary phases of childhood development, nor should they be taken as distinguishing characteristics between the child and the adult.

Dr. Montessori looked at limitations and deviations in medical, scientific terms and recognized them as abnormalities to be corrected, cured and cared for as one would care for an illness, with affection and firmness.

A child who throws temper-tantrums, for example, should be viewed as being afflicted by a behavioral deviation fostered by the environment in which the child is growing up, and by the attitudes and education of the adults who care for him. In this light, to educate a child means to care for his intelligence. By recognizing the child's limitations and deviations we can help him remove them, rather than accept them and adjust to them. Ignoring the beginning of a deviation in a small child invites the strengthening of that same deviation into adulthood.

The understanding of the principles based on rationality and the application of educational techniques (mostly correct verbalizations) are the two essential characteristics of an intelligent educator who cares to prepare a natural, healthy environment in which the child may grow up.

One must be aware that exposing a child to the wrong environment brings out the worst behavior. Conversely, exposing the child to a healthy psychological environment produces healthy attitudes and a rational behavior.

Our efforts in fostering intelligence in the children are not in vain if we hold rationality as the standard, reason as the tool of achievement and non-contradiction as the only authority.

How can we cope with the temper-tantrums of a small child such as a two-year-old? Small children are typically unable to express clearly the origin of their frustrations. A temper-tantrum of a small child may reflect many different reasons and may be the result of a number of circumstances, each requiring a different treatment. An overly tired child often throws a temper-tantrum to express his frustration simply because he feels he is having to stay awake. Discomforts produced by thirst, hunger, restrictive clothing, environment, heat or small sores, are often expressed by small children through tantrums of frustration directed at the nearest adult.

Before deciding what technique or verbalization to use in dealing with a small child's temper-tantrum, we must take time to observe and identify clearly the origin of the frustration. There is an appropriate verbalization and action for each situation. In observing objectively the behavior of the child, one can discover what action is most appropriate for eliminating a deviation at the time when it first arises.

VERBALIZATION EXAMPLE #1

A small child enters the supermarket with his mother and sees streams of wrapped candy-balls colorfully dangling in front of him. He wants them and begins by whining and begging.

LESS RATIONAL	MORE RATIONAL
Child (age 3) Mommy, may I have these candy-balls?	*Child* (age 3) Mommy, may I have these candy-balls?
Mother They are bad for your teeth. We don't want them.	*Mother* They are bad for your teeth. We don't want them.
Child Yes, I want them, I want them!	*Child* Yes, I want them, I want them!
Mother Stop it! I said no!	*Mother* You really like those candy-balls, don't you?
Child (Crying and kicking his feet.) I want those candy-balls.	*Child* Yes.
Mother If I get some, you'd have to save them until we go out to the car, OK?	*Mother* I can buy something for you that does not hurt your teeth later on, or I can take you out of the store, into the car where we can talk about this, but I will not put up with a temper-tantrum. Shall we go talk about your behavior or shall we go on and see if I can find something else for you?
Child OK.	*Child* (Calmed down) OK. Let's look for something else.

VERBALIZATION EXAMPLE #2

Mother and child are at home, at bed-time. Here is an opportunity for the parent to describe events in story form. The small child has displayed tantrums on various occasions before. Here is a perfect time to heal that deviation by working with the child when his emotions are at rest.

Mother

Tonight I want to tell you a story about you and me. Remember when we were at the supermarket this morning?

Child

Yes.

Mother

What happened there, when you saw the candy-balls? You wanted me to buy them, didn't you?

Now, look at what I am drawing on this piece of paper.

Here is this child, and his mommy going happily into the store. Suddenly, the child begins to whine and cry and kick his feet. He is throwing a temper-tantrum in front of all the people. He says: "Mommy, get the candy-balls! I want the candy-balls!" What did Mommy do? She said: "Oh no, these are not good for your teeth. We cannot have them." Did the little boy stop his temper-tantrum and understand his Mommy?

Child

No.

Mother

What did Mommy do, then?

Child

She asked the little boy to go back to the car and talk about this.

Mother

That's right. And I was so pleased to find out that it was not necessary to go back to the car and that we could get something else, a little surprise that does not hurt the teeth. But the next time (anticipation), when we go to the supermarket, will you start whining and fussing again?

Child

No.

Describing events in story form, with humor, if possible, is very effective for a healthy relationship between child and adult. Such condition does not create fear, anxiety or guilt. It's a technique designed to give the child time to think things through and see himself acting, reacting and interacting with all the consequences, without being totally involved, while still holding the power to change the entire picture, if necessary.

It is possible that no matter what skill and efforts one may put forth in preventing the child to reach the temper-tantrum point, the frustration fit is unavoidable. Once the adult and the child reach the confrontation point, it is important that the child get the clear message that in a confrontation between adult and child, the child must inevitably yield. The adult will still have the opportunity to describe events in story form to the child and reconstruct the scene of the confrontation and re-assess it together. In this way, the child will have a chance to develop proper judgment and not just fight the adult.

IX
Eliminating Problems With Property/Sharing

Children are possessive by nature. They identify with having objects of their own. This sense of possession is part of the child. The baby is possessive. Biologically, his very survival depends on having access to the objects and the people from which pleasure is derived.

Property, however, is not mere possession. While possession is primarily an emotional issue, property arises with social context and the regulation of social interaction. Property is associated with the intellectual, philosophical organization of a society. Therefore, when we talk about property, we inevitably talk about the right to property or the right to own and possess.

If one lived on a desert island, the question of right to property would be meaningless, but the emotion of possessiveness or non-possessiveness would still be felt and relevant, because possessiveness is based on desire and desire is a human emotion inseparable from the individual, whether in or out of a society.

The adult in charge of educating the child must understand clearly the difference between property right and possession. The two concepts are not interchangeable. Possession does not automatically imply property, for example. Property must be validated in a social context, hopefully a rational one, while possession is self-evident.

Our social structure recognizes that anything that we make our own is an extension of our identity. One can validate such an extension and from this validation we derive the concept of property right.

Possession, on the other hand, is founded on a more sensorial level. It is a feeling that arises when one comes in contact with a desirable object. The feeling of possession arises spontaneously based on the psychological condition of the individual. The act of possessing does not indicate ownership, it simply denotes the fact of having, right or wrong as it may be.

Can children have the right to property? This is a disturbing question, because we understand that property arises from the social structure. In a rational society, property is recognized and identified as an inalienable extension of one's physical existence, one's life. Thus the body is rightfully the property of the individual. So are the clothes and the other possessions for which the individual has worked or exchanged goods in order to have.

A rational form of education cannot take place without a clear understanding of the distinction between the concept of property and the concept of possession.

In defending his possessions, a child often acts as though he was defending his property right. In fact, a child is responding to a feeling: the fear of losing his possession. If, as a teacher or an adult, we are not able to distinquish between the two concepts, we are very likely to grant a child a status that he does not have. By the sanction we tacitly grant, emotionally the child may soon recognize that he is at the same level of the adults.

For example, a three-year-old can intimidate his parents about the use of his lunch box because he takes the position (emotionally) that the object is *his* and he can do as he pleases with it, as though it was his property. The reality is that the lunch box is in his possession, but it is not, in fact, the child's property. If we as adults are not able to distinguish possession from property, we inevitably grant children more status than they deserve, or even wish to have.

EXAMPLE OF VERBALIZATION

A child bangs and tosses his lunch box. The teacher reprimands him and reminds him that the lunch box should be treated carefully and with respect. The child retorts without concern that the lunch box is his and he can do as he pleases.

LESS RATIONAL

Teacher
Let's carry the lunch box with care. You don't want to break it, do you?

Child (age 5)
I don't care. It's just a lunch box.

Teacher
Don't you care what happens to your lunch box? If you break it, your parents will have to buy another one.

Child
I want a new one. I don't even like this one. I don't care if it breaks.

Teacher
But it is not right to ruin this one to get a new box.

Child
This is my lunch box and I can do anything I want with it.

Teacher
You are giving a very bad example to the other children and I won't permit this behavior.

MORE RATIONAL

Teacher
Let's carry the lunch box with care. You don't want to break it, do you?

Child (age 5)
I don't care. It's just a lunch box.

Teacher
I don't think your parents appreciate the way you treat this lunch box. I expect you to carry it properly and care for it. I'll ask your parents what they think of it being banged and tossed around. Then we can decide what is the best way to care for it.

Child
I don't care and my parents won't care either about this lunch box.

Teacher
In that case, *I* care about it and I will not permit you to abuse it while you are in my class. Which do you prefer, to use it carefully or shall I keep it for you?

Child
I'll use it carefully.

In this example, the rational verbalization is based on the concept that the child does not own his lunch box, he merely has the possession, the use of it. The teacher reminds the child of the fact that his parents are really the owners of the lunch box. The teacher on the less rational side does not name the exact issue and allows the child to initiate an argument that involves the advantages and disadvantages of caring for one's lunch box. In the end, our teacher must resort to some authoritarian precept in order to close the argument.

Sharing, too, is a problem based on the psychological make-up of an individual. Related to the feeling of possession, sharing stems from another desire. One wants to share, spontaneously, when one values another person. Learning to share, however, may have its roots in fear. You must have heard people say to their children, particularly to those who cling possessively to their toys, how important it is that they learn to share.

What precisely is meant by "learning to share?" Usually, adults imply that sharing is hard to practice (like altruism). They usually put a lot of effort in teaching children to overcome their possessiveness by learning to share, whether they like it or not.

Self-sacrifice is thus looked at as a necessary ingredient of the act of sharing and it is viewed as desirable, moral and a virtuous act. In reality, nothing could be further from the truth. Forced sharing is not virtuous. Contrary to all that was taught to us, forced sharing is neither desirable nor moral.

Have you looked at this closely? When we teach children to learn to share, what do we imply? We imply that it is not the nature of the child to share. We assume that sharing has to be taught or else the child will develop into a greedy, selfish, exclusive, separate individual.

The concept of property right is a conceptual social standard that is acquired by the individual. It does not arise spontaneously, like the emotion of possessiveness or greed. Property right is a standard that must be taught.

One way of teaching these concepts is to separate property right from possessiveness. Never confuse the emotion of possession with the concept of property right. The two are entirely different. The acknowledgment of possessiveness as a natural emotion is the beginning of understanding of the concept of property right.

A child personalizes objects and people because a child may have learned that security, gratification and power all come from possession. In a rational form of education, the adult would make sure that the child understands his/her emotional needs and can separate them from what is rational and objective.

How can we help children become more rational in dealing with possessiveness? The following principles ought to be considered in dealing with the emotion of possessiveness:

a) Possessiveness is an emotion. It arises spontaneously to indicate the level of psychological security and rational abstractions of an individual.

b) Possessiveness, like all emotions, must first be understood without acceptance or rejection. When one has been raised in an atmosphere of some degree of fear of losing, of not being worthwhile, or of not being loved enough, possessiveness is the natural consequence of that environment. By understanding the whole dynamic of it, one can observe possessiveness for its destructiveness and be free of it.

c) Property right is a conceptual social standard that should be based on rationality as the only absolute means of regulating it.

d) Sharing can never be forced. Sharing is the opposite emotion of possessiveness. It arises spontaneously as the result of a healthy, self-confident, psychologically secure human being. Sharing cannot be taught, nor can it be practiced. Sharing is the correct emotion responding to psychological maturity, independence and mental health.

Once established, these principles may be taught to children by setting up the physical and psychological conditions to help them achieve mental health, self-esteem and psychological security. By achieving psychological security, we are achieving rationality. The problems of sharing and possessiveness come to an end of their own accord, without force, without practicing anything, without sacrificing anything.

Typical techniques that are most suitable for working out problems in sharing and possession are:

- anticipation
- relating values
- verbalization of feelings
- dramatization
- providing choices of behavior
- naming issues

A teacher should understand that the application of principles and techniques to class management is an art that will continue to be refined as long as the teaching profession continues. Parents already know that their job can never be considered done, no matter how old their children are.

X
Dealing With Manipulation, Lying and Pilfering

Manipulation is a form of disrespect. So are lying and pilfering. All these activities are, broadly speaking, defense mechanisms and, as such, must all have their roots in fear. A child becomes disrespectful towards people and their property when he understands, erroneously, that the obstacle to his success and his happiness is the adult.

It is with this sense of fear and lack of self-esteem that a child justifies all disrespect. The cure of disrespect is self-confidence and psychological security. By removing fear and insecurity, the child achieves happiness and success without having to lie and without having to sneak and pilfer.

Adults, more often than not, are interested in moralizing. Our roots in the traditional system justify the teaching of ethical values through indoctrination. This is a practice that has had profound damaging effects on the development of human intelligence. Indoctrination, when successful, produces obedient, God-fearing citizens who, like well trained dogs, may perform the motions of civilized people, while their minds are dull, fearful and unable to make rational judgments in new situations.

When children are raised with guilt, accused of being evil for lying, sneaking and pilfering, the message they get is not, contrary to what many educators might think, a newly found understanding of ethical values, rather the confirmation that the adults are their enemies. Often, instead of abstracting that lying, manipulating and pilfering are wrong, irrational ways of relating, these children learn the wrong lesson: they learn that their trouble comes from having been poor liars, or for having done a bad job at manipulating and pilfering. Next time they'll try harder.

Educators face a great challenge when they try to reach a child who has made a habit of manipulating, lying and cheating. They must find a way to have a trustworthy relationship with such a child and they must ultimately turn that child's abstractions around. That's not an easy task.

Most children grow up with an erroneous concept of respect. It is common to associate respect with fear of authority. While children who fear authority often give the impression of being obedient, polite and respectful as adults like them to be, frequently, in the absence of authority, these children violate all social rules. Even more commonly, children raised under the rule of thumb, who remain consistently well-behaved and law-abiding, develop an inimical, gnawing craving for power.

These are the people who have learned to identify success with authority and self-esteem with power over others. These are the future adults who will perpetuate self-righteousness and use power to teach the concept of respect to the new generations. These are not the healthy, rational people of tomorrow that we want our children to grow up to be.

Is there a form of respect that does not depend on authority, fear, or images? When we can understand the concept of respect in this light, we understand what respect really is. True respect has its roots in admiration, not in fear or images.

No amount of lecturing, punishments and repression is going to eliminate behaviors like arguing, manipulation, lying and stealing. A child who is set on this road has learned that there is only one emotion one must listen to: fear. He can only respond to authority and fear. This child has never understood the value of admiration, he has never been taught to appreciate the values of rational, non-contradictory living and admire those who live rationally.

It is our goal as teachers to challenge the children's set way of thinking about respect and disrespect and educate them to see the consequences of living rationally and irrationally.

Manipulation, lying and pilfering suggest that the individual is insecure. He must come out ahead, one way or the other, in order to feel successful and worthwhile. Thus, the basic psychology of this person is selfishness in its evil connotation, i.e. gain at the expense of others. (Selfishness in its moral connotation would be self-gain at nobody else's expense.)

137

A child psychologically secure and mature for his age would have no reason to develop patterns of manipulation, lying and pilfering. But security about one's own competence at living is acquired with great difficulty, through a complex process of environmental messages from the meaningful adults in charge of educating the child.

Learning to observe objectively and scientifically the whole dynamics of disrespect is part of the awareness and attention we must give in order to solve this problem rationally.

A small child takes whatever he wants. Being sensorial, i.e., responding primarily to sensory stimuli, he is emotionally and intellectually immature. We can see a sign of maturity in the development of a child precisely when, confronted with opportunities for gaining at other people's expense, the child makes the connection that what belongs to others makes others suffer, if it is taken without their consent. This concept of empathy for other people's feelings develops gradually, but steadily, in normal children. At the same time, it is a concept that can be easily distorted through informal education.

The home and school environments provide unlimited possibilities to either enhance or hinder the emotional and intellectual development of a child. After all, how many of us, without reciting useless regulations, can really explain why a child should not take a few cookies from the cookie jar, if no one sees him; or why should Jim admit that he is the one who took Sally's new pencil sharpener, although no one saw him?

We know it to be a fact that lying is always directed by fear. We know that a child lies precisely because it is in his self-interest to do so. Clearly, at times, in telling the truth the child may be punished and meet with disapproval.

VERBALIZATION EXAMPLE #1

A child pokes someone and says he didn't do it. The teacher witnesses the event, yet the child's fear of punishment or loss of image prompts that child to deny his action.

LESS RATIONAL

Teacher
Did you poke H.?

Child (age 3-9)
No, I didn't.

Teacher
You are not being honest about it. Now, tell me the truth. Did you or did you not poke him?

Child
No, I didn't!

Teacher
Now, that's a lie! I saw you do that to H. I want you to sit aside!

MORE RATIONAL

Teacher
I saw you poke H. Has H. done something to upset you?

Child (age 3-9)
Yes. He makes ugly faces. I don't like him.

Teacher
What do we do when someone in the classroom makes ugly faces at us?

Child
We tell the teacher.

Teacher
Yes. We do not hurt anyone. We do not poke them with pencils or anything. Will you remember to come and talk to me if it happened again next time?

Child
Yes.

Teacher
I hope H. will accept your apologies. You had better tell him that you are sorry about it and that you will not poke him again.

VERBALIZATION EXAMPLE #2

On the playground the teacher sees Robert kick Ted with anger. Ted comes crying to the teacher to complain about Robert. Now Robert is mortified and his only defense is denial.

LESS RATIONAL	MORE RATIONAL
Ted (age 7) (crying) Robert kicked me in the leg and it hurts!	*Ted* (age 7) (crying) Robert kicked me in the leg and it hurts!
Teacher Let's get some ice for your leg. Come and sit here to calm yourself. Karen, will you go to the class refrigerator and get the ice pack?	*Teacher* Come and sit down here. Let me see your leg. It looks like a bad bruise. Let's put an ice pack on it. Karen, will you go to the class refrigerator and get the ice pack?
Karen (age 9) Yes, right away.	*Karen* (age 9) Yes, right away.
Teacher Why did you kick Ted?	*Teacher* It seems to me that Robert was very upset with you.
Robert (age 7) It was an accident.	*Ted* We were just playing and he kicked me.
Ted No, it wasn't. He kicked me on purpose.	*Teacher* You rest and calm down. I'll talk to him.
Robert It was an accident.	You kicked Ted in the leg very hard.
Teacher I saw you kick him, and you were very upset.	*Robert* (age 7) It was an accident.
Robert No, It was an accident!	*Teacher* I saw you kick him on purpose and with anger.

140

Teacher
You are not telling the truth. I saw you kick him.

Robert
It was an accident!
It was an accident!

Teacher
You may very well go sit aside, both for kicking and for lying!

Robert
It was an accident.

Teacher
I am sorry, but when I see a person who loses his temper and kicks the children, I always ask that person to sit aside to calm down and then talk to me later.

(Later, when all emotions have subsided.)

Teacher
You must have been pretty upset when you kicked Ted.

Robert
He was teasing me.

Teacher
What was he saying?

Robert
He was saying I couldn't run as fast and that I was acting like a sack of potatoes.

Teacher
Did that make you very angry?

Robert
Yes.

Teacher
Is that when you lost your temper and kicked him?

Robert
Yes.

Teacher
What do we do when someone teases us?

Robert
We can come and speak to you about it.

Teacher
Yes, we cannot kick and hurt someone at school. When someone teases you, I will talk to that person. But you must not hurt him. Is that agreed?

Robert
Yes.

In a relationship based on fear, it is inevitable that there are going to be images to be protected. One cannot face the truth when there are images to be protected. Lying is a means of survival for such a person; it cannot be eradicated unless the person is assured that the truth will not carry a penalty.

What are the feelings of the child who keeps defending himself by lying ("It was an accident! It was an accident!")? What is the predominant emotion of that child? Obviously, fear. He is afraid that if he is discovered to have kicked another child on purpose (instead of by accident) he will surely be punished.

In lying, the child is hoping to remain emotionally invisible by creating an image of innocence. If that form of manipulation works, he will have been rewarded for being crafty and hypocritical. Unfortunately, if the adults see through this ploy, as most of us usually do, all the accusations and punishments inflicted for lying do not usually produce the elimination of craftiness and hypocrisy. On the contrary, through punishment and disapproval we often provide a better justification for the child to become convinced that the problem is not lying, but how skillful one becomes at it.

Through the correct verbalization of feeling, on the other hand, the adult has the opportunity to interact with the innermost part of the child. His craftiness and attempted hypocritical behavior is exposed with dignity. Respect is re-established when we say something like this:

"Perhaps you were very angry when you kicked Ted."
"Perhaps you had a very good reason for kicking Ted."
"Perhaps you think you will be punished for kicking him."

If the child answers "Yes" to any of these statements, you have been able to remove fear from the relationship. Once the relationship of trust and care is established, the child will have less and less reasons for lying.

It is erroneous to think that one ought to be truthful in order to be virtuous. The truth is not hard to tell if fear is removed. If one does not have the need to lie, all that is left is the truth. To be completely free from the need to lie is where intelligence is.

What we say about lying applies to pilfering or stealing. The emotional nature of the small child is to possess. When the small child experiences pleasure from toys or from delicious foods, he wants that pleasure repeated. That desire in the small child is very strong. It is biologically built-in for survival's sake. The understanding of that emotion is part of educating the child.

A small child often takes what he wants and makes it his by virtue of possessing it. Though this is necessary for the purpose of survival (the small child is physically dependent on others), as he grows up he must learn that *taking* is not the normal and rational mode of procuring pleasure for oneself.

QUESTION AND ANSWER DIALOGUE

Student Teacher

What can I say to a child in my class who pilfers a bunch of rubber bands and puts them in his pocket? I see him do this and when I confront him with the fact, he just denies it all.

Mr. A

We said before that the issue is not lying, in this case. We want first to build a relationship of trust. Consider the case in which one child kicked another.

Student Teacher

How do we prevent that behavior from continuing?

Mr. A

We do want to break this pattern. We don't just build a relationship of trust, of psychological security and stop there. A relationship based on trust and security is a relationship where the child and adult are visible to each other, where there is no anonymity.

To have such a relationship we must know the feelings of the child very well and verbalize them. We could verbalize the child's feelings along these lines:

Teacher

You like these rubber bands, don't you?

Child (age 6)

Yes.

Teacher

Which of these is your favorite?

Child

I like this thin one the best.

Teacher

This long one is my favorite. If I were to shoot this one, it would probably go the farthest.

144

Child

I like to tie them together.

Teacher

Do you have rubber bands at home?

Child

No, I don't. My mother never buys any.

Teacher

You would like to have these, wouldn't you?

Child

Yes.

Teacher

Is that why you put them in your pockets?

Child

Yes.

Teacher

Can we make an agreement?

Child

Yes.

Teacher

I'll talk to your mother and see if she can get you some rubber bands of your own. You put these back in the box that is on my desk. Let's make a list of the kinds of rubber bands you'd like your mother to get for you.

Child

OK.

Verbalizations of feelings like these do not *condone* pilfering and do not *repress* desire through guilt or fear. The issue is not really the rubber bands, but self-esteem. The issue is learning to regard others who are in relationship with us without antagonism, but intelligently and with understanding.

Student Teacher

What about the child who takes things from the classroom without having a particular reason for it? This is a child who does not have a pattern. You can never tell what he might take next. There is no pattern to it. It could be a little piece of Montessori equipment here, a pencil there, a few erasers, and small personal objects that belong to other children.

Mr. A

This is a child who is definitely psychologically insecure. One of the ways this child has associated with gaining security and success, obviously, is by acquiring objects that belong to others. To possess objects is symbolically interpreted as becoming successful and happier. Obviously this is a pattern of irrational behavior.

Most of us were taught to meet irrational behavior emotionally, without a clear plan, without a clear understanding of human relationship. In most cases we react to it with *disapproval*. We inevitably create a relationship based on fear. As teachers, or parents, we often automatically follow these steps when we must cope with irrational behavior in children:

a) Disapprove of the behavior
b) Teach the lesson by lecturing
c) Punish to make sure the lesson sticks.

The educator does not really fulfill one's professional role unless a situation like this is brought to a level of normalization. Surely this is a child suffering from a classic deviation, in desperate need for help. No amount of disapproval, lecturing and punishment will ever "cure" this child.

Unfortunately, most of us are ill equipped to help normalize a child like this. We often believe that only expert psychologists can provide the solution to the problem.

Experience will tell us that children biologically and genetically healthy (i.e. children who do not suffer from congenital mental imbalances or brain dysfunctions) can still acquire irrational abstractions from the environment (home and school) where they are being educated. Deviations such as lying and pilfering are likely to be environmentally acquired and are best treated by providing the opportunity for intelligent and rational relationships.

An adult who cares for the mental health of a child will take time to observe what in fact encourages and sustains a deviation and what makes irrational behavior obsolete. Any adult, parent or teacher, can become a scientific observer, driven, not by personal emotions, but by objectivity. You do not have to acquire a psychology degree in order to educate children rationally, but you must commit yourself to the facts of reality and not to wishful thinking or self-serving images.

In dealing with lying and pilfering, the adult committed to rationality as the main goal of education should follow these steps:

a) Acknowledge how important such behavior must be
b) Establish trust (no condoning, but no punishment)
c) Establish mutual visibility

How do we deal with a child who has formed the habit of taking anything he wants whenever he feels the urge to possess?

a) WE MUST ACKNOWLEDGE THE IMPORTANCE OF HIS BEHAVIOR.

Teacher
You like Marvin's eraser, don't you?

Ken (age 5)
Yes.

Teacher
Would you like to take it home with you and keep it?

147

Ken

Yes.

Teacher

Do you think your mother could buy you one just like this?

Ken

Yes.

b) ESTABLISH TRUST (NO CONDONING, BUT NO PUNISHMENT).

Teacher

You know, Ken, when you wish to have something that belongs to others, you must ask permission before you can have it. What happens if you take things that belong to other people without their permission?

Ken

I get punished.

Teacher

How do you get punished?

Ken

My Mom tells my Dad. He yells at me and spanks me.

Teacher

Do you get caught every time?

Ken

No. Not really. I get caught very *few* times.

Teacher

What do you think is the worst thing that can happen to you if I find out that you take things from the classroom and from the other children?

Ken

I don't know. Maybe, you'll tell my parents.

c) ESTABLISH MUTUAL VISIBILITY.

Teacher
I won't do that, if you make an agreement with me.

Ken
What's that?

Teacher
I want you to agree that everyday, before going home, you'll come to me voluntarily and let me check your pockets and lunch box and that I won't find anything that belongs to other people.

Ken
OK.

As the child relates daily with this teacher in mutual understanding, trust and visibility, he learns that he can spend days without the need to pilfer. Each day the teacher solemnly states something like this: "I am so happy to see that Ken's pockets and lunch box do not have anything in them that belongs to someone else. It looks to me that Ken has become a very responsible person."

Everyday the teacher confirms Ken's success. His classmates see him with renewed friendship, and Ken enjoys a new reputation. He experiences the pleasure of personal normalization and of rational relationships in action.

Like a nurse in the hospital, Ken's teacher has cared for the child as though he was afflicted by an illness. Confident that by creating a relationship based on affection and trust the child would heal himself, this teacher has done the necessary work to prevent the irrational behavior to continue.

Without the need for disapproval, without punishment or force, Ken became aware that he could act differently. We cannot force someone to act rationally, just like doctors and nurses cannot force patients to be healthy. We can only remove the obstacles and allow that which is rational and healthy to prevail.

Student Teacher

What about the concept of loyalty? A child who sees another child steal something may report it to the teacher. Such a child is being disloyal to his friend. He may even become very unpopular for reporting other people's wrong doing all the time. I have such a child in my classroom. On one hand I am glad to know what is going on in the classroom; on the other, I see that this child is hated for reporting everyone's wrong move to me. Should I not encourage loyalty and friendship among the children?

Mr. A

Loyalty to irrationality is part of irrationality. Surely we do not want to encourage it. Perhaps we should inquire in the motive for reporting anything. Why does one report wrong doing? When you see your neighbor's house being burglarized, what do you do?

Student Teacher

You report it to the authorities.

Mr. A

That is the sense of responsibility we admire. That is what we want a child to learn, isn't it? There is a sense of loyalty only if in a group of people who are out to do something wrong together, one agrees to go along and then, for self-gain at the expense of the group, he turns against them and reports them to the authorities.

The traditional classroom (very rarely the Montessori classroom) lends itself for this type of scenario. The students are often made to feel as though there is a war going on: the class as a group on one side against the adults and the authorities on the other. Individual students can feel confused about their allegiance.

In a rational form of education, a teacher is aware of this phenomenon. Our goal remains unchanged. We are not in the classroom merely to see that the academic subjects are learned, we are in the classroom to see that correct thinking is developed and thus that intelligence prevail.

A child who consistently reports on his peers is gaining and losing something. While he may be reporting to us someone else's irrational behavior that needs correcting, his self-appointed "guardian angel" position may itself be the symptom of a deviation in need of attention. To observe dispassionately such behavior we ought to ask ourselves: "What does he gain when he reports to us other people's wrong doings? And what is he willing to lose?"

Often, a child like this is in desperate need of approval and recognition. What he probably gains is the adult's recognition at the expense of popularity amongst his peers.

Closing Remarks on Scientific Pedagogy and Individual Initiative

The traditional method of education, widespread as it is in both private and public schools, destroys intelligence subtly and overtly. The traditional system demands that students conform. Thus, they themselves become part of the system. It is not by reforming the system that human beings will be liberated from the pressures and dullness of conformism, but by allowing the system to perish.

Unfortunately, and ironically, it is often the system's intellectual opponents who help it stay alive. The best teachers and the most creative educators provide it with constant and innovative revitalization. Even many Montessorians, perhaps the most intellectually well-equipped to fight the traditional system among all educators, frequently compromise their ideological integrity and accept traditional standards to measure their own progress. They may advocate self-paced learning for young pre-kindergarten students, but recommend "real schools" for elementary students; they may decide that grouping students by chronological age is a more efficient way of giving lessons than to tailor their presentations to individual differences; they may be unprepared to gauge students' progress objectively without resorting to using standardized achievement tests.

All serious educators share the same wishes and aspirations. They want to see a world dominated by understanding, peace, happiness — a world where the professional status of education ranks as high as that occupied by science and medicine.

However, if such a status has not been achieved, it is due to a faulty philosophy of education. The failure of an educational system is the failure of the educators themselves who insist in approaching education as a *belief* instead of a science.

152

With no specific sense of direction, simply exalting general goals such as "respect for the child," "spiritual education," or "education for the whole child," many people who advocate alternative forms of education enlist in social reform movements and simply repeat pleasant-sounding platitudes endlessly.

In the field of education, people are easily divided by the *how*, the method of doing things. The *how* is belief. There is nothing more divisive for human beings than their belief, their blind faith. The stronger the belief, the deeper the division that ensues. The opposite is true of the scientific realm. The deeper the scientific knowledge, the less there is to argue about it. Can the field of education evolve to this level? Is the human race mature enough to put aside childish and sentimental beliefs?

Obviously, neither the discovery of what works nor the observation of facts can be a matter of belief. In order to achieve a form of education capable of meeting the fundamental needs of the human being, we need an objective and scientific approach to learning.

Dr. Montessori was the only educator who gave education a scientific status. She recognized that, like science, education takes place not by mere wishing, not by imposing our values and goals on the students, but by applying ourselves as "scientific observers" of the nature and needs of the human being. In Montessori education, personal capabilities — both the teacher's and the student's — reign supreme. The profound respect that Montessorians advocate for the child comes from the realization that unless the learning process is allowed to begin within the natural curiosity of the child, a teacher cannot be a guide, but a hindrance. Inculcation must be put aside to allow auto-education to flourish. With auto-education, the teacher guides each individual child through the learning process. It is in this way that punishments and rewards will naturally cease. In this way self-education means self-discovery and the child embarks on a journey that yields endless inner rewards.

With a mind open only to scientific truth, it is possible to meet the problem of right education afresh. With such a mind, objectivity and rationality — not a personal belief — would set the standards of our methodology. A great number of people all over the world hope for unity, pray for unity and believe

153

in unity. But their personal and cultural beliefs are the very barriers that impede unity. Indeed, in the great diversity of languages, philosophical thoughts and traditions, only rational thinking—the essential characteristic that separates man from all other species—remains the unifying principle of the human race.

In the objective and scientific method people from vastly different backgrounds may join their efforts and share the advantages of their discoveries. In science, the East and the West are united, because what is objectively demonstrable for one culture can never be contradicted by another. A philosophy of education based on science would provide us with a method suitable for all cultures and applicable by anybody anywhere.

What exactly can we do to develop a science of education? For one thing, certain well-known facts of reality should not be ignored by those who wish to make a difference in the field of education. Self-esteem flourishes when the individual's learning process is respected, i.e. when the student is allowed to progress at one's own pace, correct one's own errors, repeat one's work as many times as one needs in order to achieve proficiency. The traditional method consistently violates these principles. Even the so-called progressive schools—loose variations of the traditional system—tend to work with groups rather than individuals, pass and fail students and demand that students adapt to curriculum instead of scaling difficulties to meet individual's needs.

The training of Montessori teachers and the establishment of small private schools by dedicated trained individuals within the purview of their cities and neighborhoods may produce still the most long-lasting educational revolution of the century. Underestimating the capabilities of single individuals, Montessori training centers today vie for their share of government subsidies and grants designed to improve mass education. But courting revenues from government funds has proven quite unreliable many times before. More than once the direction of politics has come around full circle: what is going to be financed today might very well be what we will be fighting tomorrow.

Dependence on government favors has been a major factor in diminishing the rate of growth of the Montessori method in Europe, even during the time when Dr. Montessori was alive. The chance that European governments would incorporate the Montessori method to become the officially recognized educational system, kept Montessori and her close collaborators always hopeful that state officials would take notice and finance their endeavors. Above and beyond political factions, such financial help came often from ministers and officials on both extremes of the political spectrum — including Mussolini's fascist regime in Italy. However, no government ever incorporated Montessori as the exclusive educational system, and the Montessori method had to continue its slow growth fueled by private endowments and dedicated individuals.

The Montessori movement really became established when it was exported to the United States where, after Dr. Montessori's death in 1952, the great Montessori revival took place. Much of the credit for the expansion of Montessori in the last forty years, not only in America but around the world, must be given to individual entrepreneurs. As men and women traveled to Europe to be trained in Montessori education through the decades of the 60's, 70's and 80's, more and more small private Montessori schools appeared in North America.

Today, the combined number of Montessori schools in Italy, France, Germany, Switzerland, Holland and many other European countries probably does not exceed the number of schools one would find in a single large metropolitan U.S. city. While other countries in the world, especially those dominated by strong, centralized public school systems, have made it impossible for Montessori's individualized education to even be attempted, in the United States thousands of small and large schools (our current record indicates approximately six thousand) thrive primarily on single individuals' initiative.

Our insistence that mass education must have continued urgent attention from government has made of education a political issue. We have been trained to believe that education is an individual right (duty?) for each citizen. Millions of dollars are siphoned each year into a system designed to provide a service called education that consumers must buy, whether they like it or not.

Both the recipients of education and their dispensers are unsure about what it is exactly that they are buying or selling.

Some think each child should receive the basics (reading, writing and computing). Others say there is no education without "moral" education, without religious instruction — and there most people differ from denomination to denomination. Some educators want it all; they want good instruction in the academic subjects, they want a unified, holistic moral education, they want well-equipped, scientifically designed environments conducive to learning and well-trained teachers who approach education both as a science and a spiritual call to serve. Most educators see government as the provider and believe that government must be responsible both for the quality and the expense of the service.

By correcting these dreadful errors in our thinking, we may be able to unleash new energies and better solutions for the problems of education. If educators treat the field of education as scientists treat science, their social status would graduate to a loftier level. The creative power of individual initiative cannot be found in the unearned money of government subsidies. No amount of money and legal force placed by compulsory education today can ever match the far-flung beneficial effects that individual initiative would have if society were to place the full burden of education — not on governments — but on the single individuals!

In describing the twelve points of the Montessori method in his book *The Montessori Revolution*, E. M. Standing* stresses the importance of individual responsibility and independence of judgment as a fundamental need of the child who is being educated. Educating young children to think and live independently is exactly what is *not* happening in mass education. It is time to realize that the seeds we sow are the crops we reap. Mass education produces mass thinking; individualized education produces independent thinking.

The principle of independence guides us in the preparation of the Montessori classroom. Even very small children in an infant/toddler class are encouraged to do things for themselves

---

* E. M. Standing, *The Montessori Revolution*, New York, Schocken Books, 1966.

and to make choices. But the preparation of the physical environment is only the visible aspect of Montessori education. The invisible, yet powerful, psychological environment is truly responsible for guiding the students from subconsciousness to consciousness.

The preparation of the psychic environment is the preparation of the adults' minds. To the degree that adults value and apply objectivity and rationality in their class management, they bestow objectivity and rationality onto their students — a truly measurable and demonstrable spiritual gift.

Freedom of movement and freedom of choice, in Montessori education, are both the means and the ends of the educational process. Montessorians do not expect these qualities to remain confined within the four walls of a classroom. They expect individual children to absorb such characteristics and manifest them as adults throughout their lives. But the freedom to move and choose is valid only within the parameters of rational thinking. Any purposeless, erratic or impulsive choice is part of license, not freedom. Such behavior is recognized as a mental deficiency, rather than a sign of maturity and independence.

The spiritual preparation of the teacher must be understood in scientific pedagogical terms as the preparation of the psychological environment. Before the physical environment can be assembled, a great sense of order and clear thinking must be created in the mind of the teacher — the invisible environment.

To bring about a deep transformation of educational practices, we must begin at the individual level. The inner revolution of even a few individuals is far more important for the progress of mankind than the persuasion of the masses. Individually, we are responsible towards the children within our immediate reach, at home and at school. By beginning with ourselves and our immediate relationships, we have a real chance of success. Our individual success, even when numerically small, is not in vain. If intelligence, objectivity and rationality are sown today, the seeds of reason will undoubtedly continue to sprout amongst future generations

Index